The Painful Plough

a portrait of the agricultural labourer in the nineteenth century from folk songs and ballads and contemporary accounts

selected and edited by
ROY PALMER

foreword by
EDWARD THOMPSON

CAMBRIDGE UNIVERSITY PRESS
CAMBRIDGE
LONDON · NEW YORK · MELBOURNE

The Resources of Music Series

General Editors: *Wilfrid Mellers, John Paynter*

1. THE RESOURCES OF MUSIC *by Wilfrid Mellers*
2. SOUND AND SILENCE *by John Paynter and Peter Aston*
3. SOMETHING TO PLAY *by Geoffrey Brace*
4. MUSIC DRAMA IN SCHOOLS *edited by Malcolm John*
5. THE PAINFUL PLOUGH *by Roy Palmer*
6. THE VALIANT SAILOR *by Roy Palmer*
7. TROUBADOURS *by Brian Sargent*
8. MINSTRELS *by Brian Sargent*
9. POVERTY KNOCK *by Roy Palmer*
10. JAZZ *by Graham Collier*
11. JAZZ LECTURE CONCERT (Record and booklet) *by Graham Collier*
12. RIGS OF THE FAIR *by Roy Palmer and Jon Raven*
13. POP MUSIC IN SCHOOL *edited by Graham Vulliamy and Ed Lee*

Acknowledgements

Full source references to songs are given on p. 63. Sources of illustrations are listed on p. 64. The author and publisher would like to thank all those there listed for permission to reproduce material in this book.

Authors and publishers are thanked for permission to quote prose extracts from: W. Cobbett, *Rural Rides*, Penguin 1967; J. Burnett, *Plenty and Want*, Penguin 1968; J. & L. B. Hammond, *The Village Labourer*, Guild Books 1948; G. D. H. Cole & R. Postgate, *The Common People*, Methuen 1961; G. E. Evans, *Ask the fellows who cut the hay*, Faber 1956; W. Hudson, *A Shepherd's Life*, Methuen 1910; G. Edwards, *From Crow Scaring to Westminster*, Labour Publishing Co. 1922; J. Sage, *Memoirs*, Lawrence and Wishart 1951; M. K. Ashby, *Joseph Ashby of Tysoe*, C.U.P. 1961.

While every effort has been made to contact copyright holders, the publishers apologize if any material has been included without permission.

For assistance in the preparation of the book, the author would like to thank: Pam Bishop, for guitar chords (except songs 7 and 13); Sandra Faulkner, for guitar chords (song 13); John Swift, for guitar chords (song 7); Bob Thomson for the transcription of song 13; Katharine Thomson, for advice on the music; Librarians and staffs at Cambridge University Library, British Museum, Birmingham Reference Library, Norwich Public Library, Vaughan Williams Memorial Library; Edward Thompson, not only for his foreword but for heartening encouragement; and members of the National Union of Agricultural and Allied Workers.

Illustrations on the cover and title page were redrawn by Martin Jones from earlier originals.

Performing and recording rights are reserved and are administered by the Performing Rights Society, The Mechanical Copyright Protection Society and affiliated bodies throughout the world. Applications should be made to these bodies for a relevant licence. Failure to so apply constitutes a breach of copyright.

CAMBRIDGE UNIVERSITY PRESS
Cambridge, New York, Melbourne, Madrid, Cape Town,
Singapore, São Paulo, Delhi, Tokyo, Mexico City

Cambridge University Press
The Edinburgh Building, Cambridge CB2 8RU, UK

Published in the United States of America by Cambridge University Press, New York

www.cambridge.org
Information on this title: www.cambridge.org/9780521085120

© Cambridge University Press 1972

This publication is in copyright. Subject to statutory exception and to the provisions of relevant collective licensing agreements, no reproduction of any part may take place without the written permission of Cambridge University Press.

First published 1972
Reprinted 1976
Re-issued 2011

A catalogue record for this publication is available from the British Library

Library of Congress Catalogue Card Number: 76-187081

ISBN 978-0-521-08512-0 Paperback

Cambridge University Press has no responsibility for the persistence or accuracy of URLs for external or third-party internet websites referred to in this publication, and does not guarantee that any content on such websites is, or will remain, accurate or appropriate.

Contents

		page
Epigraph		4
Foreword		5
Introduction		6
Notes for teachers		7
List of dates		8

1. 'I was born at Barford'   9
   Bird scarers' cries (Song 1)   9

2. 'My first employer'   12
   The farmers done over (Song 2)   12
   The new-fashioned farmer (Song 3)   14
   Country hirings (Song 4)   15

3. 'I never took the Communion'   19
   The sucking pig (Song 5)   20

4. 'We labourers had no lack of lords'   22
   The labouring man (Song 6)   22
   Pity poor labourers (Song 7)   24
   The Owslebury lads (Song 8)   25

5. 'Those who owned and held the land'   28
   The honest ploughman (Song 9)   28

6. 'From crow-scarer to ploughboy'   31
   Present times, or Eight shillings a week (Song 10)   32

7. 'It was 1835'   34
   Van Dieman's Land (Song 11)   35
   The sheepstealer (Song 12)   36

8. 'I stayed on in the old home'   39
   The rigs of the times (Song 13)   40
   Poor shepherds (Song 14)   41

9. 'In 1847'   43
   Prop of the land (Song 15)   43

10. 'By the end of the sixties'   44
    The fine old English labourer (Song 16)   44

11. 'The day was 7th February, 1872'   47
    My master and I (Song 17)   49

12. 'At one place, forty-five men gave in their names'   51
    Come all you bold fellows that follow the plough (Song 18)   52

13. 'In my own county'   54
    The painful plough (Song 19)   54
    The sheep shearing (Song 20)   56

14. 'The day I entered Parliament'   59
    Three acres and a cow (Song 21)   60

15. 'As I sit here'   61
    The jolly ploughboy (Song 22)   62

Sources   63
List of records   64
Index of songs   64

Epigraph

All my life I have felt many and many a time, that the lot of the Farm Labourer has been harsher than any other Class of Workers. They were called evry sort of name – Jony Hodges, Clod hoppers, Louts, any other low term that come to there tongues, by the rest of the Workers and the Town People.

But I think that the Tiller of the soil is the highest and oldest workman of all. No one can do without him and the product of his hands. The Gold miner canot eat his gold, nor the Coal miner his coal, nor the Iron miner his Iron. All and every one is dependent upon the tiller of the Soil. He is the Father of all Workers, like the old saying has it:

> The King he governs all,
> The Parson pray for all,
> The Lawer plead for all,
> The Ploughman pay for all
> And feed all.
>
> (The King of the Norfolk Poachers)

This is, I verily believe it, the worst used labouring people upon the face of the earth. Dogs and hogs and horses are treated with more civility. (William Cobbett)

A man with the weight of many masters on him learns to be dumb, and deaf, and blind, at a very early hour in the morning. (Joseph Arch)

I should like to see the time when churches were turned into barns and parsons into threshing men. (A labourer)

All mankind has, by the original grant of the Creator, a right to pursue and take away any fowl or insect of the air, any fish or inhabitant of the waters, and any beast or reptile of the field. (Blackstone)

For 65 years, one woman, not far from my home, through her young womanhood and middle and old age, slept wakefully at nights and moved softly by day, listening always for footsteps. In 1831 her husband and brother had both been transported – one for 14 years, the other for 7 years – for their part in the riots. Till the 14 years had passed she would not let herself expect them. The one must wait for the other, she said. But at the end of that time for almost 50 years she hoped through each hour; and she died in her chair turned towards the East, because she had heard that it was out of the sunrise that travellers from Australia must come. (Sturge Gretton)

Their favourite virtue was endurance. Not to flinch from pain or hardship was their ideal. A man would say, ' 'Ole bull he comes for me, wi's head down. But I didn't flinch. I ripped off a bit o' loose rail and went for he, 'twas him as did th' flinchin'.' (Flora Thompson)

> They hang the man and flog the woman
> Who steals the goose from off the Common;
> But let the greater criminal loose
> Who steals the common from the goose.
>
> (Traditional rhyme)

Some of my Warwickshire forbears fought with Cromwell at Edgehill, and in other battles of the Civil War, against tyranny and oppression and for the liberty of the people. I expect that is where I get my fighting propensities from; fighting was in the blood, and I just harked back to those old Roundhead ancestors of mine, who struck many a brave and sturdy blow on the right side. (Joseph Arch)

One minute they're treatin' you like the fam'ly and the next minute they're treatin' you like an old work-horse that they've had the best years out of. And they'd just shoot you, I think, if they had their way. (Warwickshire farm labourer, 1971)

Foreword

When I was sixteen I was lucky enough to work as a 'farmer's boy' for eight months. I learned many things, but most of all I learned how ridiculous is the townsman's picture of the agricultural labourer as an 'unskilled' man.

The average labourer even in the early 1940s (and he had many more mechanical aids than did his grandfather, who might have sung some of these songs) had to be competent in a dozen skills. He had to manage the slow, strong, patient horses; deal with and repair harness and tackle and implements; dig ditches and lay sound drainage; cut and lay hedges; plough a straight line across erratic, undulating acres; turn his hand to the stock if the shepherd or cowman was ill or needed help; and job or improvise at carpentry, building-work, metal-work.

Even the roughest or simplest-seeming tasks require patience, strong common-sense, and a 'knack'. I wonder how many townsmen could shape a good gate-post with an axe, and set it deeply in the ground, so that it can bear the weight of a heavy gate for thirty or more years, and not lean over the first time it is knocked by a horse or wagon?

Perhaps a few townsmen could do this. But I am sure that no-one but a skilled labourer could build a corn-rick, laying each sheaf as carefully as a bricklayer, especially at the corners of the stack. A badly-built rick might easily come down in the autumn gales, and the harvest be spoiled.

This skilled worker, the field labourer, has always been underpaid and under-rewarded for his skills, and in the nineteenth century grossly so. He and his women and children also, throughout the summer months, worked excessive hours, which left little time or energy for relaxation. In order to get through these long days of heavy labour, the countryman tended to conserve his energy, walking slowly in his heavy boots over the clay, tossing the sheaves into the wagon with an unhurried, steady rhythm. Something of this deceptive slowness or steadiness was to be found also in his speech and in his songs.

The townsman sometimes mistook this slowness for stupidity. But beneath this unhurried and measured way there was often acute observation, great shrewdness, as well as constancy and uncomplaining courage in the face of hardship.

Some of these qualities come through in this collection of songs. I'm not certain that every one of the songs in this collection would have been sung by the labourers themselves; one or two of them look to me like songs written *for* or *about* the labourers by outsiders. I won't say which, since readers should try to judge this for themselves.

Undoubtedly most of the songs are authentic, in the sense that they were sung by labourers, or labourers will have enjoyed hearing them sung. Roy Palmer has assembled this collection in his capacities both as a scholar, with an unusually extensive knowledge of the collections of folk-song and of broadsheet ballads, and as a singer, who is presenting to you a tradition that is still alive. His book does not require my recommendation, and I am only here because, for some reason, he wanted the first few pages to be made up of solemn untuneful noise. As soon as you have climbed over the fence of the last introductory sentence, you will be back among the nineteenth-century fields and furrows, and the book will recommend itself.

E. P. Thompson

Introduction

This is a collection of folk songs and ballads which give a picture, from the viewpoint of the agricultural labourer, of life on the land during the nineteenth century. Historians have sometimes felt that the labourers had no means of expressing their views, other than destructive riots on the one hand or mute submissiveness on the other. The Hammonds, for example, write of the 1830s that: 'the voice of the poor themselves does not come to our ears. This great population seems to resemble nature, and to bear all the storms that beat upon it with a strange silence and resignation.' Yet, at that very time, labourers were singing, at the plough-tail, at the public house, at the fireside, not only the traditional repertoire of songs which expressed pride in their strength and skill, but ballads which expressed bitter indignation at their lot.

Some of their songs and ballads had been handed down from father to son, having originated generations earlier, and it should be remembered that certain features of country life had changed little since medieval times. Others were made up by village poets, as they often were about interesting or important events, as late as the 1880s. Many such songs, no doubt, had a short life and were then lost, but some were sufficiently cherished to enter the oral tradition. *The Owslebury lads*, for example, was made up in 1830 and turned up in a collector's notebook in 1906, having travelled for 76 years purely by oral transmission.

Another category was the broadside ballads, which were printed on small slips of paper and sold at fairs and markets in their hundreds, and even thousands. These set out to cater for the rural public and therefore to provide material which would be congenial. Much of this is worthless, but in some, the shilling hacks have been skilful enough to catch the authentic idiom of the people. Like their home-produced fellows, the broadsides sometimes enjoyed only a brief currency, but sometimes passed into the tradition.

Finally, some songs were composed in the 1870s for the labourers to sing at their meetings. They were usually to well-known tunes but, although the influence of the music-hall and the non-conformist hymnal is apparent, there is still something of the folk idiom left. These songs, like *The fine old English labourer*, were extraordinarily popular – one book of them sold 120,000 copies – for a few years only, and only a few scraps passed into the traditional repertoire.

They were traditional, however, in at least one respect: they were felt by the labourers to be their own property and to express their feelings and aspirations. Historians will sometimes feel that the picture of life which these songs give is inaccurate or erroneous. The upsurge of militancy in the 1870s, for example, is described by a recent historian as a 'revolution of rising expectations', rather in the same way as the French revolution was said to have broken out because things had begun to improve and the people, on realising that things could be better after all, rushed out to the barricades. Whatever the truth of the theory may be, the French in 1789 and the English labourers in 1872 felt that life had become intolerable and a change was imperative. The songs express what was felt to be true, and, insofar as feelings caused actions, they must be accorded the right to have existed.

Each chapter begins with an extract from the autobiography of Joseph Arch (1826–1919). Arch had the qualities which, for many, epitomise the Englishman. He was sturdy, stubborn, self-reliant, and a champion of the underdog. He was the son of an agricultural labourer who brought up his family 'without reproach, on low wages, and in hard times'. His mother was a domestic servant at Warwick Castle who inculcated in her son a hatred of oppression and a love of Shakespeare and the Bible. Both parents were proud and independent. Arch owed them much and was grateful to them all his life.

He started work at the age of nine as a crow-scarer, then became a ploughboy. At thirteen, he was driving a pair of horses and a plough and his wages had risen from 4d to 8d a day. Next, he became a stable-lad at 8s a week and by the age of sixteen, he was a mower earning 1s 6d a day. He learned hedge-cutting and became champion of England in this art. When he was twenty-one, he was a sort of contractor for mowing, draining, hedging, fence and hurdle making and an employer of up to twenty-five men.

He became known and respected as a 'steady, industrious and capable workman', but also as an advocate of the labourers' cause. Indeed, he acquired the reputation of being 'a contentious brawler, a dissenting wind-bag, and a Radical revolutionary'. From boyhood he had been indignant at the conditions of the agricultural labourers and also at the contempt in which the common people were held by the squirearchy. During the 1850s and 60s, however, the labourers seemed cowed and submissive. Arch's own lot, unlike that of his fellows, was steadily improving, but he had come to the conclusion that the only way in which conditions could be generally improved was to form a union.

In 1872, the opportunity came, apparently out of the blue. Arch was approached by a group of labourers, launched a union, and attracted a hundred thousand members within a few months. Not only were the farm labourers electrified, but the shock waves ran through the whole of England.

After a number of stirring struggles, the union went into a decline which coincided with another slump in English agriculture. The venture was, however, of great importance and it was the crowning point in Arch's career, surpassing even his election to Parliament. He lived to see the formation of a new union, which became the present National Union of Agricultural and Allied Workers, and he died in 1919 after a war which marked the end of an era in English agriculture.

When Joseph Arch was an infant, William Cobbett was touring England and writing his passionate protests at the distress of agricultural labourers. Cobbett died in 1835, when Arch was just starting work as a labourer and the two men have a number of similarities. Both were self-made and self-educated; they were practical and down to earth; they were radical-conservatives, homely and forthright but having a touch of arrogance; they were patriarchal; they were limited in ideas but passionately devoted to the popular cause.

The songs are followed by notes and commentary and extracts from a wide variety of prose sources. Finally, there are suggestions for further reading.

Notes for teachers

The Painful Plough is a source book of material for reading, singing, discussion and study, which will be of use primarily in the fields of music and of history, but also in those of social studies and English. Apart from its use in classroom and library, however, the material can be used for performance, either in a straightforward recital of songs and readings, or in a more sophisticated dramatised documentary. This might include, as available and appropriate, narration, singing, recorded interviews, dramatic scenes and visual illustration in the shape of slides (which could be based on the illustrations in the book) or film. Additional visual stimulus can be provided by exhibitions of photographs, objects borrowed from museums, and, possibly, art work.

Such a documentary provides excellent opportunities for inter-disciplinary work. When presented to pupils, it may be regarded as a piece of team teaching, to be followed up, discussed and evaluated in different ways by teachers of different subjects. It can also provide a focus for topic work and for allied work in such subjects as art, craft and movement. Finally, it can stimulate the seeking out of historical and human material in the localities of different schools. Oral reminiscences, memoirs, documents, local newspapers, archives, can shed more light on such topics as fairs and markets, poaching, agricultural crafts and techniques, tithes, enclosures, rural unrest and trade unionism. Such research, when embodied in a documentary, gives particular local relevance, which rivets an audience.

List of dates

- 1793 Wars with France began
- 1801 General Enclosure Act
- 1815 Victory over France
  Corn Laws passed
- 1816 Riots in East Anglia
- 1824 Average wage for labourers, 9s 4d a week
- *1826 Joseph Arch born*
- 1830 Labourers' Revolt
- 1832 First Reform Act
- 1834 Tolpuddle martyrs
  New Poor Law Act
- 1846 Corn Laws repealed (not effective until 1849)
- 1850 Average wage 9s 6d
- 1857 Transportation abolished
- 1870 Average wage 12s
- 1872 Warwickshire Agricultural Labourers' Union, then National Agricultural Labourers' Union formed (100,000 members by the end of the year)
- 1874 Average wage 14s
  Great lockout
- 1879 N.A.L.U. down to 20,000 members
- *1885 Arch elected M.P. (Liberal)*
- *1886 Defeated*
- *1892 Re-elected*
- 1896 N.A.L.U. ceased to exist
- *1898 Arch's autobiography published*
- 1900 Average weekly wage 15s
- *1900 Arch retired from Parliament*
- 1906 The Eastern Counties Agricultural Labourers' and Small Holders' Union formed (forerunner of present farm workers' union)
- *1919 Arch died*
- 1976 Minimum wage for agricultural workers, £36.50 a week

1

'I was born at Barford'

I was born at Barford, in Warwickshire, on 10th November 1826. I was a youngster of nine when I began to earn money. My first job was crow-scaring, and for this I received fourpence a day. This day was a twelve hours one, so it sometimes happened that I got more than was in the bargain, and that was a smart taste of the farmer's stick when he ran across me outside the field I had been set to watch. I can remember how he would come into the field suddenly, and walk quietly up behind me; and, if he caught me idling, I used to catch it hot.

Song 1 *Bird scarers' cries*

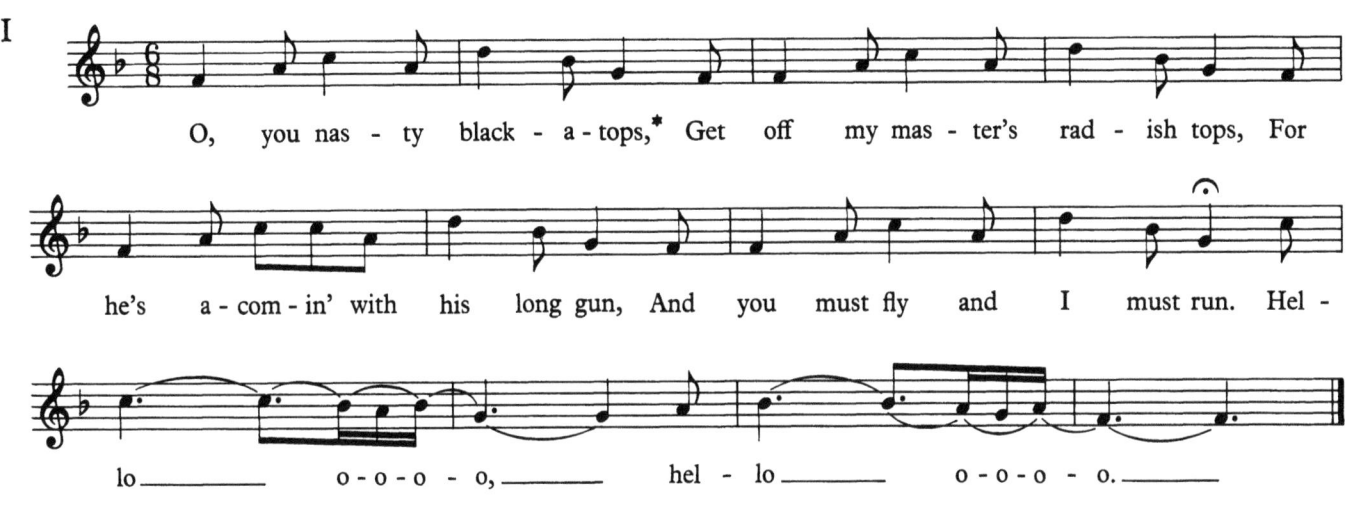

O, you nas-ty black-a-tops,* Get off my mas-ter's rad-ish tops, For he's a-com-in' with his long gun, And you must fly and I must run. Hel-lo o-o-o-o, hel-lo o-o-o-o.

* Black-a-tops: blackbirds.

A-way, you black dev-ils, a-way, A-way, you black dev-ils, a-way, You eat too much, you drink too much, You car-ry too much a-way, a-way.

III

Hey, shoo all the birds. Out of my master's ground into Tom Tucker's ground, Out of Tom Tucker's ground into Tom Tinker's ground. Hey, shoo all the birds. Kraal! Hoop!

† This and the following bar are repeated as required.

Second time, add: Out of Tom Tinker's ground into Luke Coles's ground.

Third time, add: Out of Luke Coles's ground into Bill Veater's ground.

Fourth time, add: Out of Bill Veater's ground, back to my master's ground.

IV

Gee, hallo, hallo, blackie cap, Let us lie down and take a nap. Suppose our master chance to come? You must fly and I must run. Gee hallo, hallo, hallo! Gee hallo, hallo, hallo!

Sowing and harrowing (left); harvest (right)

Frightening birds off the crops was the usual occupation for children in the country from very early times until within living memory. William Cobbett, who was born in 1766, started his working life in this way: 'My first occupation was driving the small birds from the turnip seeds, and the rooks from the peas. When I trudged afield, with my wooden bottle and my satchel over my shoulders, I was hardly able to climb the gates and stiles, and, at the close of day, to reach home was a task of infinite labour.'

Medieval wood-carving (misericord) in the church at Ripple, Worcestershire, showing boys scaring birds

Further reading

Quotations from Joseph Arch at the beginning of each chapter are from his autobiography. This was published first in 1898, under the title of *Joseph Arch: the story of his life*. An abridged edition was published by MacGibbon and Kee, London, in 1966, as *The autobiography of Joseph Arch*.
See also P. Horn, *Joseph Arch*, The Roundwood Press, Kineton 1971.

W. Cobbett, *Autobiography*, ed. W. Reitzel, Faber, London 1967.
Bob Copper, *A song for every season*, Heinemann, 1971.
P. Horn, *The Victorian country child*, Roundwood Press, 1974.

2

'My first employer'

My first employer was a big, burly man, fairly well-to-do. He came to grief, however, through his extravagance. He did not look after his business properly, and, to make matters worse for himself, he married a London lady who would be very gay. There were too many farmers and farmers' wives of this sort in my youth, and it is my candid opinion that there are more of them about now than there ever were.

Farmers' wives nowadays are ashamed to go to market to sell their eggs and butter as they used commonly to do. They want to play the piano, dress fine, make calls and ape the gentry, and of course the farms will not stand it. How can they? And the farmers too want to hunt, and shoot, and play the fine gentleman at ease.

Then, when these would-be swells find their cash run short, they cry out that it is the labourers who are extravagant and shiftless, who want too high a wage, who do too little work, and are bringing the land to ruin!

Song 2 *The farmers done over*

Come all you swaggering farmers of courage stout and bold And listen to my ditty, the truth I will unfold; For these full twenty long years past you've had a roaring trade, Now they all pull long faces and are dreadfully dismayed. So pity us poor servants, who run at every call, We give no satisfaction and our wages are so small.

* Continue with guitar chord indicated until next symbol.

2 When the farmers to the market went, on hunters they did ride
  And then their daughters rode in gigs to run on by their side.
  When they came up to the inn, the ostler they did call:
  If he delayed a moment, how they would swear and bawl.

3 The landlord in alarm to the door did run straightway,
  Crying, Ostler, be attentive to these gentlemen, I pray,
  For if my business you neglect, your wages I will pay,
  For in my service, I declare, you shall no longer stay.

4 Well, next a waiting maid is called his daughters to attend,
  To take her to a room, my boys, then for a glass they send,
  Then her false wig she takes off, to the barber's for to go,
  Then in the glass she views herself from very top to toe.

5 The large straw bonnets they stand up a-poking out like thus,
  That nothing but a donkey could give to them a buss;
  Their petticoats so narrow and waists bound up so tight,
  And they look in a glass to see if they are walking right.

6 Now the times they are altered, they can't keep up their pride;
  They now must go on foot, my boys, where once they all did ride;
  If at the inn you should call in, you'll see the farmers there;
  Instead of wine to drink they've only a glass of beer.

7 In eighteen hundred and sixteen, of land they were so keen,
  They rode about the country, the like was never seen;
  From one hundred to two hundred their rents they did advance,
  But now without a fiddle it makes them for to dance.

8 To go unto the statutes it is but little use;
  Our wages are so small, my boys, they hardly find us shoes.
  Besides the ugly frowns and the curses we do get,
  The farmers they do swear that they are running into debt.

9 And they who are not broke, my boys, have got a dreadful crack,
  Their visages are very long, their looks are very black.
  So sudden was the change that it made them all to stare
  As bad as any wild beast you ere saw at a fair.

Song 3 *The new-fashioned farmer*

2. A good old-fashioned, long grey coat the farmers used to wear, sir,
   And old Dobbin they would ride to market or to fair, sir;
   But now fine geldings they must mount to join all in the chase, sir,
   Dressed up like any lord or squire before their landlord's face, sir.

3. In former times, both plain and neat, they'd go to church on Sunday,
   Then to harrow, plough or sow they'd go upon a Monday.
   But now, instead of the plough tail, o'er hedges they are jumping;
   Instead of sowing of their corn their delight is in fox-hunting.

4. The farmers' daughters used to work all at the spinning wheel, sir;
   Now such furniture as that is thought quite ungenteel, sir.
   Their fingers they're afraid to spoil with all such kind of sport, sir,
   And sooner than a mop or broom they'd handle a piano-forte, sir.

5. Their dress was always plain and warm, when in their Sunday clothes, sir;
   Besides, they had such handsome cheeks, as red as any rose, sir.
   But now they're frilled and furbelowed, just like a dancing monkey;
   Their bonnets and their great black veils would almost fright a donkey.

6. When wheat it was a guinea a strike the farmers bore the sway, sir;
   Now with their landlords they will ride upon each hunting day, sir.
   Besides, their daughters, too, must join the ladies to the hall, sir;
   The landlords say, we'll double the rents, and then their pride must fall, sir.

7. It's all this confounded pride has brought them to reflection;
   It makes poor servants' wages low and keeps them in subjection.
   Let's pray that hungry bellies may be filled when they are empty;
   And where a servant gets ten pounds I wish he may get twenty.

Song 4 *Country hirings*

Come all you bold young country lads and listen unto me
And if I do but tell the truth, I know you will agree.
It's of the jolly farmers who servants want to have,
For to maintain them in their pride and be to them a slave.
Stand up for wages, servant men, To the hirings when you go,
For you must work all sorts of weather, Cold and wet and snow.

2 The farmer and his wife in bed so snug and warm can lie,
   While you must face the weather, both cold and wet and dry.
   For the rents they are heavy and the taxes they are high
   And we must pull down the wages, the farmer he does cry.

3 The farmers, twenty years ago, could rents and taxes pay,
   But now their pride is very high, and increases every day,
   Which makes the landlords raise the rent and the farmers for to scold
   All on the poor young servant lad and rob him of his gold.

4 The farmer and the servant together used to dine,
   But now they're in the parlour with their pudding, beef and wine,
   The master and the mistress, their family all alone,
   And they will eat the beef, my boys, while we may pick the bone.

5 The farmers' daughters used to dress both neat and plain and brown,
   But now with bustles, furbelows and flounces to their gowns
   They do get dressed like dandy Bess, more fitter for the stage,
   Which makes the landlords raise the rents and put them in a rage.

6 The description of our living, I'm sure it is the worst,
   We have coarse brown bread, rye pudding, and mouldy old pie crust,
   While all the masters they do live as you shall understand
   On butter and good cheese, my boys, and the fat from off the land.

During the late eighteenth century farms were growing in size and prosperity as a result of enclosures.‡ The war with France, at least until 1812, stimulated the demand for corn, and the farmers prospered still more.

The increased wealth of the farmers disturbed the close relationship they had once had with farm labourers, who had normally lived at the farm as members of the family until they married. The labourer, instead of being part of the household, was obliged to fend for himself. The farmer, instead of sharing the work of his men, became more of a manager and employer.

The new prosperity also led to changes in the way of life of the farmers, changes which the labourers considered to be needless extravagance. A jingle published in *The Times* in 1822 summed up the difference between the old farmers and the new:

> 1722
> Man to the plough;
> Wife to the cow;
> Girl to the sow,
> Boy to the now,†
> And your rents will be netted.
> 1822
> Man tally-ho;
> Miss piano;
> Wife silk and satin;
> Boy Greek and Latin;
> And you'll all be Gazetted.*

When hard times came for agriculture, the labourers felt that they were obliged to bear a disproportionate share of the burden, as the two songs indicate. According to Cobbett, 'this accursed system' changed the farmers into 'a series of mock gentlefolks', while it 'ground the labourers down into real slaves'. 'Why do not the farmers feed and lodge their work-people, as they did formerly? Because they cannot keep them upon so little as they give them in wages.' (*Rural rides*, p. 227.)

The statute or hiring fairs were held for the purpose of engaging farm labourers, many of whom contracted for a year at a time. These fairs are no longer held, but their names often survive (for example, the Statute Fair at Luton, still held every September). They were held usually between September and Christmas, but some took place on the 1st of May. So that their trade might be seen at a glance, labourers wore some emblem of their calling. The ploughman sported a piece of whipcord, for example, and the shepherd, a tuft of wool.

There follow two eye-witness accounts of statutes (or mops, as they are called in parts of the Midlands):

‡ See Further Reading list overleaf.
† Now: barn.
* A similar rhyme was still felt to be true in 1843 (see G. M. Trevelyan, *English social history*, Penguin Books, Harmondsworth 1967, p. 485). Gazetted means listed as bankrupt.

Hunting the hare

Statutes and Mops I, 1827

The 'Statute' I first attended was held at Studley, Warwickshire, at the latter end of September. On arriving, between twelve and one o'clock, at the part of the Alcester road where the assembly was held, the place was filling very fast by groups of persons of almost all descriptions from every quarter. Towards three o'clock there must have been many thousands present. The appearance of the whole may be pretty accurately portrayed to the mind of those who have witnessed a country fair; the sides of the roads were occupied with stalls for gingerbread, cakes, &c., general assortments of hardware, japanned goods, waggoner's frocks, and an endless variety of wearing apparel, suitable to every class, from the farm bailiff, or dapper footman, to the unassuming ploughboy, or day-labourer.

The public-houses were thoroughly full, not excepting even the private chambers. The scene out of doors was enlivened, here and there, by some wandering minstrel, or fiddler, round whom stood a crowd of men and boys, who, at intervals, eagerly joined to swell the chorus of the song ... The servants were, for the most part, bedecked in their best church-going clothes. The men also wore clean white [smock] frocks, and carried in their hats some emblem or insignia of the situation they had been accustomed to or were desirous to fill: for instance, a waggoner, or ploughboy, had a piece of whipcord in his hat, some of it ingeniously plaited in a variety of ways and entwined round the hatband; a cowman after the same manner had some cow-hair; and to those already mentioned there was occasionally added a piece of sponge; a shepherd had wool; a gardener had flowers, &c. &c.

The girls wishing to be hired were in a spot apart from the men and the boys, and all stood not unlike cattle at a fair waiting for dealers. Some of them held their hands before them, with one knee protruding (like soldiers standing at ease), and never spoke, save when catechised and examined by a master or mistress as to the work they had been accustomed to; and then you would scarce suppose they had learned to say anything but 'Ees, sur', or 'No, sur', for these were almost the only expressions that fell from their lips. Others, on the contrary, exercised no small degree of self-sufficient loquacity concerning their abilities, which not unusually consisted of a good proportion of main strength, or being able to drive or follow a variety of kinds of plough. Where a master or mistress was engaged in conversation with a servant they were usually surrounded by a group ... this in some, perhaps, was mere idle curiosity, in others, from desire to know the wages asked and given, as a guide

A hiring fair in the 1820s

to themselves ... They appeared to require a certain sum for wages, without reference to any combination of circumstances of the state of the times; ... they would stand for some time and hear reasons why wages should be more moderate, and at the conclusion ... the usual answer was 'Yo'll find me yarn it, sur', or 'I conna gue for less'.

When a bargain is concluded on at a 'Statute', it is the custom to ratify it immediately, and on the spot, by the master presenting to the servant what is termed 'earnest money', which is usually one shilling...

The contract arises upon the hiring: if the hiring be general, without any particular time limited, the law construes it to be hiring for one year; but the contract may be made for a longer or shorter period. Many farmers are wary enough to hire their servants for fifty-one weeks only, which prevents them having any claim upon that particular parish in case of distress...

When the hiring is over, the emblems in the hats are exchanged for ribbons of almost every hue. Some retire to the neighbouring grounds to have games at bowls, skittles, or pitching, &c. &c., whilst the more unwary are fleeced of their money by the itinerant Greeks and black legs with E.O. tables*, pricking in the garter, the three thimbles, &c. &c. These tricksters seldom fail to reap abundant harvests at the Statutes. Towards evening each lad seeks his lass, and they hurry off to spend the night at the public-houses ... The rooms of the several houses are literally crammed, and usually remain so throughout the night...

The time for Statute-hiring commences about the beginning of September, and usually closes before old Michaelmas-day, that being the day on which the servants enter their new services, or, at least, quit their old ones. Yet there are some few Statutes held after this time, which are significantly styled 'Runaway Mops': one of this kind is held at Henley-in-Arden, on the 29th of October, being also St Luke's fair. Three others are held at Southam, in Warwickshire, on the three successive Mondays after old Michaelmas-day. To these Statutes all repair, who, from one cause or another, decline to go to their new places, together with others who had not been fortunate enough to obtain situations.

The Statutes I have visited for the purpose of obtaining these particulars are Studley, Shipston-on-Stour, and Aston-Cantlow, all in Warwickshire. I observed no particular difference either in the business or the diversions of the day, but Studley was by far the largest. At Stratford-on-Avon, and some other places, there is bull-roasting. (W. Pare of Birmingham in Hone's *Everyday book*, vol. III, cols. 174ff (1838 edition).)

*E.O. was a fairground gambling game.

Statutes and Mops II, 1917

The first Mop in Warwick market place was on 12th October. Then there were two more on the next two Saturdays after. We stood in a row in the market place. The waggoners had a little bit of whipcord in their button hole. The cowman had a bit of hair off a cow's tail and the shepherd 'ud have a bit of wool. I was a plough lad; I had a bit of whipcord. The farmer used to come up to us and say, 'Oh, will you come and work for me?' If you said 'yes' he give you the shillin' and you'd start next morning. You had to be there twelve months. You had to go twelve months without any wages.

The last year of the hirings was 1917. I had my shillin' but I got talking to some people afterwards and they said: 'The farmer ent worth tuppence.' So, next day, I got the shillin' off my father and I sent it back to the farmer so I didn't go. (Reminiscence of Mr Lusby of Wellesbourne in an interview with Roy Palmer, 1971. Mr Lusby was born in 1906 and started work at the age of 11 in 1917.)

Further reading

William Cobbett, *Rural rides*, Penguin Books, Harmondsworth 1967.
Margaret Baker, *Discovering English fairs*, Shire Publications, Tring n.d.
R. Palmer and J. Raven, *The rigs of the fair*, Cambridge, 1976.
John Masefield, *Grace before ploughing*, Heinemann, London 1966 (ch. 4 describes a hiring fair at Ledbury).
Thomas Hardy, *Far from the madding crowd*, 1874 and many modern editions (ch. 6 describes a hiring fair, which also figures in the film of the book).
W. E. Tate, *The English village community and the enclosure movements*, Gollancz, London 1967.
Riot and be hanged: Ely and Littleport, Cambridgeshire and Ely Education Committee, 1971.

Haymaking

3

'I never took the Communion'

I never took the Communion in the parish church in my life. When I was seven years old [1833] I saw something which prevented me once for all. One Sunday my father was going to stop to take the Communion, and I, being a boy, had of course to go out before it began. So I went out of church, closed the door, placed my eye at the keyhole and peeped through, and what I saw will be engraved on my mind until the last day of my life.

First, up walked the squire to the communion rails; the farmers went up next; then up went the tradesmen, the shopkeepers, the wheelwright, and the blacksmith: and then, the very last of all, went the poor agricultural labourers in their smock frocks. They walked up by themselves; nobody else knelt with them; it was as if they were unclean.

A popular anti-tithe story, that of the woman who offered her tenth child to the parson, is illustrated by this Staffordshire pottery group of about 1825. The parson is wearing the "cocked hat and bushy wig" mentioned in song 5

Song 5 *The sucking pig*

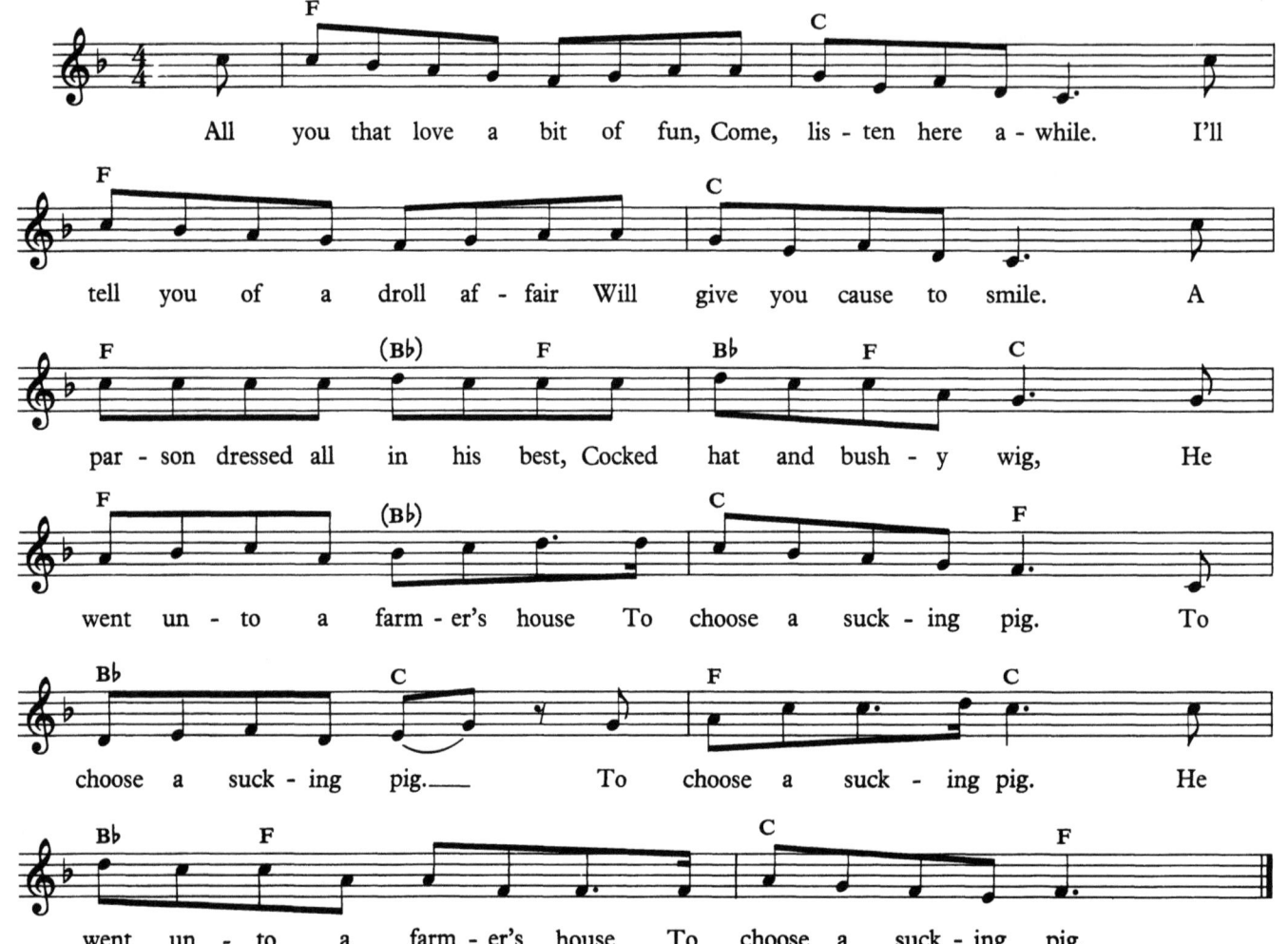

2 Good morning, says the parson,
   Good morning, sir, to you.
   I've come to claim a sucking pig,
   You know it is my due.
   Therefore I pray go fetch me one
   That is both plump and fine,
   Since I have asked a friend or two
   Along with me to dine.

3 Then in the sty the farmer goes,
   Among the pigs so small,
   And chooses for the parson
   The least among them all.
   But when the parson saw the same,
   How he did ramp and roar;
   He stamped his foot and shook his head
   And almost cursed and swore.

4 O then, replied the farmer,
   Since my offer you refuse,
   I pray, sir, walk into the sty
   There you may pick and choose.
   Then in the sty he ventured
   Without any more ado;
   The old sow ran with open mouth
   And at the parson flew.

5 O then she caught him by the coat
   And took off both the skirts,
   Then ran her head between his legs
   And threw him in the dirt.
   The little pigs his waistcoat tore,
   His stockings and his shoes;
   The farmer cried, you're welcome, sir,
   I hope you'll pick and choose.

6 At length they let the parson out,
   All in a handsome trim.
   The sow and pigs so neatly in
   The dirt had rolled him.
   Away the parson scampered home
   As fast as he could run;
   The farmer almost split his sides
   With laughing at the fun.

7 The parson's wife stood at the door,
   Awaiting his return,
   And when she saw his dirty plight
   Into the house she turned;
   My dear, what is the matter,
   Where have you been, she said.
   Get out, you bitch, the parson cried,
   For I am almost dead.

8 Go fetch me down a suit of clothes,
   Go fetch them down I say,
   And bring me my old greasy wig
   Without any more delay.
   And for the usage I received
   All in the cursed sty
   I ne'er shall relish sucking pig
   Until the day I die.

Arch's autobiography is full of accounts of the petty tyranny exercised in the village of Barford by the rector and his wife. In addition to the resentment which labourers felt at this they disapproved of parsons acting as magistrates and enforcing laws which were considered unjust. Finally, clergy were unpopular because they levied tithes.

A tithe was one-tenth of all produce: the tenth piglet from the litter, the tenth fruit, the tenth sack of corn – but not (as the illustration satirically suggests) the tenth child. There was a great deal of bad feeling over tithes. One farmer sent to the parson to warn him that the turnips were to be got up. When the parson's man arrived with his cart, he was solemnly presented with one turnip, the farmer having pulled only ten. More seriously, a parson at Radford (near Barford) was murdered because of his insistence on collecting tithes (see *Joseph Ashby of Tysoe*).

After the Tithe Act of 1836, a rent-charge was substituted for payment in kind, but friction continued into this century (see *Ask the fellows*). *The sucking pig* probably dates from the eighteenth century but it was sung at least until the end of the nineteenth. The poorest pig of the litter was traditionally reserved for the parson; hence the Cheshire saying, 'Poor and peart [lively] as the parson's pig': the thinnest piglet being the most active.

Further reading
M. K. Ashby, *Joseph Ashby of Tysoe, 1859–1919*, Cambridge University Press, London 1961.
G. E. Evans, *Ask the fellows who cut the hay*, Faber, London 1966.

4

'We labourers had no lack of lords'

We labourers had no lack of lords and masters. There was the parson and his wife at the rectory. There was the squire, with his hand of iron over-shadowing us all. At the sight of the squire the people trembled. He lorded it right feudally over his tenants, the farmers; the farmers in their turn tyrannised over the labourers; the labourers were no better than toads under a harrow.

Some of the farmers' wives were in sympathy with the people, but only a very few of them. I wish I could say as much for their husbands. What kindliness they possessed was like the other side of the moon in relation to the earth, it was always turned away from the agricultural labourer.

They impressed themselves on me as taskmasters and oppressors, and my heart used to burn within me when I heard of their doings, and when I saw how the men who toiled so hard for them were treated like the dirt beneath their feet.

Song 6 *The labouring man*

You Eng-lish-men of each de-gree, A mo-ment lis-ten un-to me, To please you all I do in-tend With these few lines I'm goin' to pen. From day to day you all may see The poor are frowned on by de-gree By them, you know, who nev-er can Do wi'-out the lab'-ring man.* Let Eng-land do the best she can, She

* Labouring man: agricultural labourer.

can't do wi'-out the lab'-ring man. Old Eng-land al-ways leads the van, But nev-er wi'-out the lab'-ring man.

2. In former days you all do know
   A poor man cheerful used to go,
   Both neat and clean, upon my life,
   All with his children and his wife;
   And for his labour, it was said,
   A fair day's wages he was paid,
   But now to live he hardly can;
   May God protect the lab'ring man.

3. When Bonaparte and Nelson, too,
   And Wellington at Waterloo
   Were fighting both by land and sea,
   The poor man gained the victory.
   Their hearts were cast in honour's mould,
   The soldiers and the sailors bold,
   And every battle, understand,
   Was carried by the lab'ring man.

4. Now if the wars do rise again
   And England be in want of men,
   They'll have to search the country round
   To find the lads that plough the ground,
   Who harrow the ground and till the wheat,
   And every danger boldly meet.
   For England always leads the van,
   But never wi'out the lab'ring man.

A cartoon of 1831

Song 7 *Pity poor labourers*

2. There's many poor lab'rers to work they will go
   Either hedging or ditching, to plough or to sow,
   And many poor fellows are used like a Turk:
   They do not get paid fair for half a day's work.

3. And many poor lab'rers, I'm sorry to say,
   Are breaking of stones for eighteenpence a day.
   Bread and water's the fare of the poor lab'ring man,
   While the rich they can live on the fat of the land.

4. Some pity the farmers, but I tell you now,
   Pity poor lab'rers that follow the plough.
   Oh pity poor children half-starving and then
   Divide every great farm up into ten.

5. There's many young fellows you'll see every day
   For snaring a hare they are banished away
   To Van Dieman's Land* or to some foreign shore
   And their wives and their children are left to deplore.

6. There's many a farmer that's making a fuss,
   While the poor and the starving can scarce get a crust.
   Do away with their hounds and their hunters so gay
   And give the poor lab'rers a little fair play.

7. Fair play is a stranger these many years past,
   And pity's bunged up in an old oaken cask,
   But the time's fast approaching, it's very near come,
   When *we*'ll have the farmers all under our thumbs.

* Van Dieman's Land: Tasmania (see Song 11).

Song 8 *The Owslebury lads*

2. Oh then to Winchester we were sent, our trial for to take,
   And if we do have nothing said, our council we shall keep.
   When the judges did begin, I'm sorry for to say,
   So many there was transported for life and some was cast to die.

3. Sometimes our parents they comes in all for to see us all,
   Sometimes they bring us some baccy or a loaf that is so small,
   Then we goes into the kitchen and sits all round about,
   There is so many of us that we're very soon smoked out.

4. At six o'clock in the morning our turnkey† he comes in
   With a bunch of keys all in his hands tied up all in a ring,
   And we can't get any further than back and forward the yard;
   A pound and a half of bread a day, and don't you think it hard?

5. At six o'clock in the evening the turnkey he comes round,
   The locks and bolts they rattle like the sounding of a drum,
   And we are all locked up all in the cells so high
   And there we stay till morning whether we lives or dies.

6. So now to conclude and finish my new song,
   I hope you gentlemen round me will think that I'm not wrong,
   And all the poor in Hampshire for rising of their wages –
   I hope that none of our enemies will ever want for places.

* Owslebury: a small village near Winchester (colloquially pronounced Usselbry). † Turnkey: gaoler or warder.

Hard times

As to the produce of this valley [in Wiltshire], it must be at least ten times as great as its consumption, even if we include the three towns [Salisbury, Heytesbury, Warminster] that belong to it. I am sure I saw enough produce in five or six of the farm-yards, or rick-yards, to feed the whole of the population of the twenty-one parishes. But the infernal system causes it all to be carried away: Not a bit of good beef, or mutton or veal, and scarcely a bit of bacon is left for those who raise all this food and wool. The labourers here *look* as if they were half-starved... For my own part, I am really ashamed to ride a fat horse, to have a full belly, and to have a clean shirt upon my back, while I look at those wretched countrymen of mine; while I actually see them reeling with weakness; when I see their poor faces present me nothing but skin and bone, while they are toiling to get the wheat and meat ready to be carried away to be devoured by the tax-eaters. I am ashamed to look at these poor souls, and to reflect that they are my countrymen; and particularly to reflect, that we are descended from those, amongst whom 'beef, pork, mutton and veal, were the food of the poorer sort of people' (*Rural rides*, p. 337).

The standard of life from 1800 to 1834 sank to the lowest possible scale; in the south and west wages paid by employers fell to 3s to 4s per week, augmented by parochial relief from the pockets of those who had no need of labour; and insufficient food left its mark in the physical degeneracy of the peasantry. Herded together in cottages, which, by their imperfect arrangements, violated every sanitary law, generated all kinds of disease, and rendered modesty an unimaginable thing... compelled by insufficient wages to expose their wives to the degradation of field labour, and to send their children to work as soon as they could crawl... [the labourers] would have been more than human if they had not risen in an insurrection which could only be quelled by force. They had already carried patience beyond the limit where it ceases to be a virtue. (From R. E. Prothero. *The pioneers and progress of English farming*, 1888, quoted in J. Burnett, *Plenty and want*, p. 30.)

In their classic work, *The village labourer*, J. L. and Barbara Hammond describe with passionate indignation the effects of enclosures during the late eighteenth century and the distress on the land during the early nineteenth century, particularly between 1815 and 1830. Their story ends soon after the beginning of Joseph Arch's life, but it explains the bitter hatred which labourers, including Arch, sometimes felt towards the farmers.

After Waterloo, they write, England experienced fifteen years of peace:

Yet at the end of all this time the conquerors of Napoleon found themselves in a position which they would have done well to exchange with the positions of his victims... The English labourer alone was poorer; poorer in money, poorer in happiness, poorer in sympathy, and infinitely poorer in horizon and in hope. The riches that he had been promised by the champions of enclosure had faded into something less than a maintenance. The wages he received without land had a lower purchasing power than the wages he had received in the days when the wages were supplemented by common rights...

This was not part of a general decline... The lives of the judges, the landlords, the parsons, and the rest of the governing class were not become more meagre but more spacious in the last fifty years... The agricultural labourers whose fathers had eaten meat, bacon, cheese, and vegetables were living on bread and potatoes. They had lost their pigs and fowl, they had ceased to brew their beer in their cottages. In their work they had no sense of ownership or interest... Men and women were living on roots and sorrel; in the summer of the year 1830 four harvest labourers were found under a hedge dead of starvation, and Lord Winchelsea, who mentioned the fact in the House of Lords, said this was not an exceptional case. The labourer was worse fed and worse housed than the prisoner, and he would not have been able to keep body and soul together if he had not found in poaching [see pp. 34 ff] or in thieving or in smuggling the means of eking out his doles and wages.

The Hammonds go on to describe the explosion which took place among agricultural labourers in 1830, which has since been described as the last labourers' revolt. This was a widespread movement which began in Kent and moved through Sussex, Hampshire, Berkshire, Wiltshire, Dorset, and then into the Midlands. The labourers, with allies among craftsmen and small farmers, rioted, demanded small sums of money, broke threshing machines, burned down workhouses and called for higher wages, under the leadership of a mythical hero, Captain Swing. The disturbances were ruthlessly repressed by the authorities. In the country as a whole 644 men were hanged and a score jailed. Some 500 men were sent to Botany Bay and Van Dieman's Land.

At the village of Owslebury, near Winchester, John Boys, a small farmer, supported the labourers. He was tried for being in a mob which extorted money from a steward, but acquitted. On the orders of the Attorney General, he was tried by another court, convicted, and sentenced to seven years' transportation. Out of 345 prisoners at Winchester, 2 were hanged, 131 transported and 65 imprisoned with hard labour.

When he was writing *A shepherd's life*, W. H. Hudson spoke to people who remembered the trials:

It was when the trial was ended, when those who were found guilty and had been sentenced were brought out of the court-house to be taken back to prison, and from all over the Plain and from all parts of Wiltshire their women-folk had come to learn their fate, and were gathered, a pale, anxious, weeping crowd, outside the gates. The sentenced men came out looking eagerly at the people until they recognised their own and cried out to them to be of good cheer. "Tis hanging for me', one would say, 'but there'll perhaps be a recommendation to mercy, so don't you fret till you know.' Then another: 'Don't go on so, old mother, 'tis only for life I'm sent.' And yet another: 'Don't you cry, old girl, 'tis only fourteen years I've got, and maybe I'll live to see you all again.' And so on, as they filed out past their weeping women on their way to Fisherton Jail, to be taken thence to the transports in Portsmouth and Plymouth harbours waiting to convey their living freights to that hell on earth so far from home. Not criminals but good, brave men were these.

Further reading

J. Burnett, *Plenty and want*, Penguin Books, Harmondsworth 1968.

J. L. & B. Hammond, *The village labourer*, Guild Books, London 1948, 2 volumes.

E. J. Hobsbawm and G. Rudé, *Captain Swing*, Lawrence and Wishart, London 1969.

W. Hudson, *A shepherd's life*, Methuen, London 1910.

E. P. Thompson, *The making of the English working class*, Penguin Books, Harmondsworth 1969.

E. J. Hobsbawm, *Industry and empire*, Penguin Books, Harmondsworth 1969.

A pictorial commentary on the Labourers' Revolt of 1830–1

5
'Those who owned and held the land'

Those who owned and held the land believed that the land belonged to the rich man only, that the poor man had no part nor lot in it, and had no sort of claim on society. They thought that when a labourer could no longer work, he had lost the right to live. Work was all they wanted from him. It was what he was made for, to labour and toil for his betters, without complaint, on a starvation wage. When no more work could be squeezed out of him, he was no better than a cumberer of other folk's ground, and the proper place for such as he was the churchyard.

Song 9 *The honest ploughman*

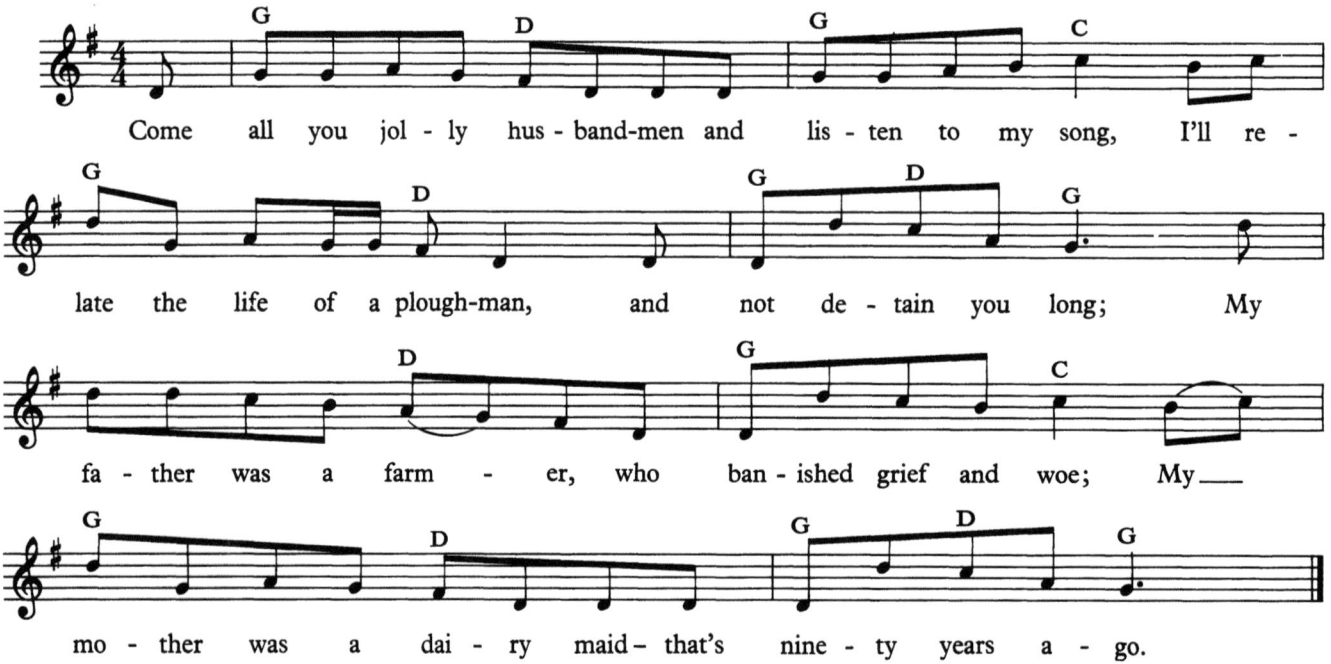

Come all you jolly husbandmen and listen to my song, I'll relate the life of a ploughman, and not detain you long; My father was a farmer, who banished grief and woe; My mother was a dairy maid – that's ninety years ago.

2 My father had a little farm, a harrow and a plough,
  My mother had some pigs and fowls, a pony and a cow;
  They didn't hire a servant, but they both their work did do,
  As I have heard my parents say, just ninety years ago.

3 The rent that time was not so high, but far as I will pen,
  For now one family's nearly twice as big as then was ten;
  When I was born my father used to harrow, plough, and sow,
  I think I've heard my mother say, 'twas ninety years ago.

4 To drive the plough, my father did a boy engage,
  Until that I had just arrived to seven years of age;
  So then he did no servant want, my mother milked the cow,
  And with the lark I rose each morn to go and drive the plough.

5 When I was fifteen years of age, I used to thrash and sow,
   I harrowed, ploughed, and harvest-time I used to reap and mow;
   When I was twenty years of age, I could manage well the farm,
   I could hedge and ditch, and plough and sow, or thrash within the barn.

6 At length when I was twenty-five, I took myself a wife,
   Compelled to leave my father's house, as I have changed my life;
   The younger children in my place, my father's work would do,
   Then daily as an husbandman to labour I did go.

7 My wife and me, tho' very poor, could keep a pig and cow,
   She could sit and knit, and spin, and I the land could plough;
   There nothing was upon a farm at all, but I could do,
   I feel things very different now – that's many years ago.

8 We lived along contented, and banished pain and grief,
   We had not occasion then to ask parish relief;
   But now my hairs are grown quite grey, I cannot well engage
   To work as I had used to do – I'm ninety years of age.

9 But now that I'm ninety years of age, and poverty do feel,
   If for relief do go, they shove me in a Whig Bastille,*
   Where I may hang my weary head, and pine in grief and woe,
   My father did not see the like, just ninety years ago.

10 When a man has laboured all his life, to do his country good,
   He's respected just as much when old as a donkey in a wood,
   His days are gone and past, and he may weep in grief and woe,
   The times are very different now, to ninety years ago.

   * Whig Bastille: workhouse (see below p. 30).

The skeleton at the plough

THE
Saucy Plough Boy.

Ryle & Co., Printers, Monmouth-ct Bloomsbury

COME all you pretty maidens gay,
   And listen unto me,
Will you wed with a saucy ploughboy
   Whose heart is light and free.

For the plough boys they are merry lads
   To the fields they'll hast away,
While the pretty maids are milking,
   Or making of sweet hay.

I'll rise in the morning early,
   And trip along with joy,
While the small birds sing so charming
   I'm a saucy ploughing boy.

See the lambs how they are sporting,
   And we will kiss and toy,
I've silver in my pocket love,
   A saucy ploughing boy,

I am kind and free hearted,
   No care shall me annoy,
I'm frolicsome and easy.
   A saucy farmer's boy.

They love for to be dancing,
   They're jovial and so free,
Come along you saucy plough boy,
   No other lads for me.

But mark returning home again,
   When a milking you have been
The meadows look so charming love,
   Will you wear the gown of green.

Do you tease me, you can please me,
   This damsel she would cry,
And with my saucy plough boy
   I mean to l've and die.

Broadside ballad of the mid-nineteenth century

The workhouse was the most feared and hated institution which existed during the nineteenth century. The scene in Dickens' novel where Oliver Twist asks for more is one of the most famous in English literature. It was the New Poor Law of 1834 which set up the 'Whig Bastilles' and 'created more embittered unhappiness than any other statute of modern British history'. (*Industry and empire*.)

Agricultural labourers often looked back to better times in the past and they certainly preferred the earlier system of 'parish relief'.

There is indeed evidence that the eighteenth-century Poor Law . . . became more generous, and when poverty became catastrophic, during the hard years of the middle 1790s, the country gentry went dead against the grain of economic theory in the 'Speenhamland System'. In its most ambitious versions this set out to establish a minimum wage based on the cost of bread, if necessary subsidised out of the rates. (*Industry and empire*.)

The New Poor Law . . . set up three Commissioners to establish 'union' workhouses by means of a compulsory union of parishes for that purpose, and in order to 'deter' applicants who were presumed to be probably only work-shy, to enforce the following principles through elected Boards of Guardians: (i) No relief except within a workhouse to the able-bodied; (ii) Such relief to be 'less-eligible' than the most unpleasant means of earning a living outside; (iii) Separation of man and wife to prevent childbearing.

The Act was applied forthwith to the South of England, extinguishing the Speenhamland system, which had reduced that part of the country to extreme abjectness. It met with little resistance. . .

In 1836 the new Poor Law Commissioners, known everywhere among the workers as 'The Three Bashaws [Pashas] of Somerset House', . . . were ready to turn their attention to the industrial areas, in which, though the Speenhamland system did not exist in the same form they saw a 'laxity' in the granting of relief to the distressed of which they disapproved almost as much.

The approved unpleasantness of relief was to be secured by offering it only in the workhouse – the hated 'Bastille', as the poor soon learned to call it – and in addition keeping those who accepted the 'workhouse text' in a contrite frame of mind by means of a low diet, a severe discipline, and a rigid segregation of the sexes which separated man and wife. . .

William Cobbett and a tiny band of left-wing Radicals and old-fashioned Tories fought side by side in vain against the Bill. Their opponents, even the most fanatical, were not inhuman monsters, but rather ruthless logicians, who believed that in the end their strong medicine would benefit the sufferers. (*The common people*, pp. 276–7.)

Further reading

E. Hobsbawm, *Industry and empire*.
G. D. H. Cole and R. Postgate, *The common people, 1746–1846*, Methuen, London 1961.
J. J. & A. J. Bagley, *The English Poor Law*, Macmillan, London 1966.
M. E. Rose, *The English Poor Law, 1780–1930*, David and Charles, Newton Abbot, 1971.
N. Longmate, *The Workhouse*, Temple Smith, 1975.

6
'From crow-scarer to ploughboy'

From crow-scarer to ploughboy was my next step, with an accompanying increase in wages of twopence a day. When I was between twelve and thirteen years of age [1838–9] I could drive a pair of horses and plough my own piece. It was a proud day for me when I drove my first pair and got eightpence a day wage. This kind of work is generally called 'gee-oh-ing'. There was a wealthy banker and Justice of the Peace in the village [and] he took me into his stables, made me a sort of stableboy, and gave me eight shillings a week to start with. In time my wages went up to nine shillings a week. I went on working in the stables until I was about sixteen [1842], and then I started mowing for the same banker. He used to pay me eighteenpence a day for what he would have had to pay another man half-a-crown. I felt the injustice of this treatment more and more keenly, but I dared not speak out – the time for *that* had not come, and I could not risk the loss of my earnings, for my father was in receipt of only eight shillings a week just then.

THE RIVALS.

A cartoon of 1843

Song 10 *Present times, or Eight shillings a week*

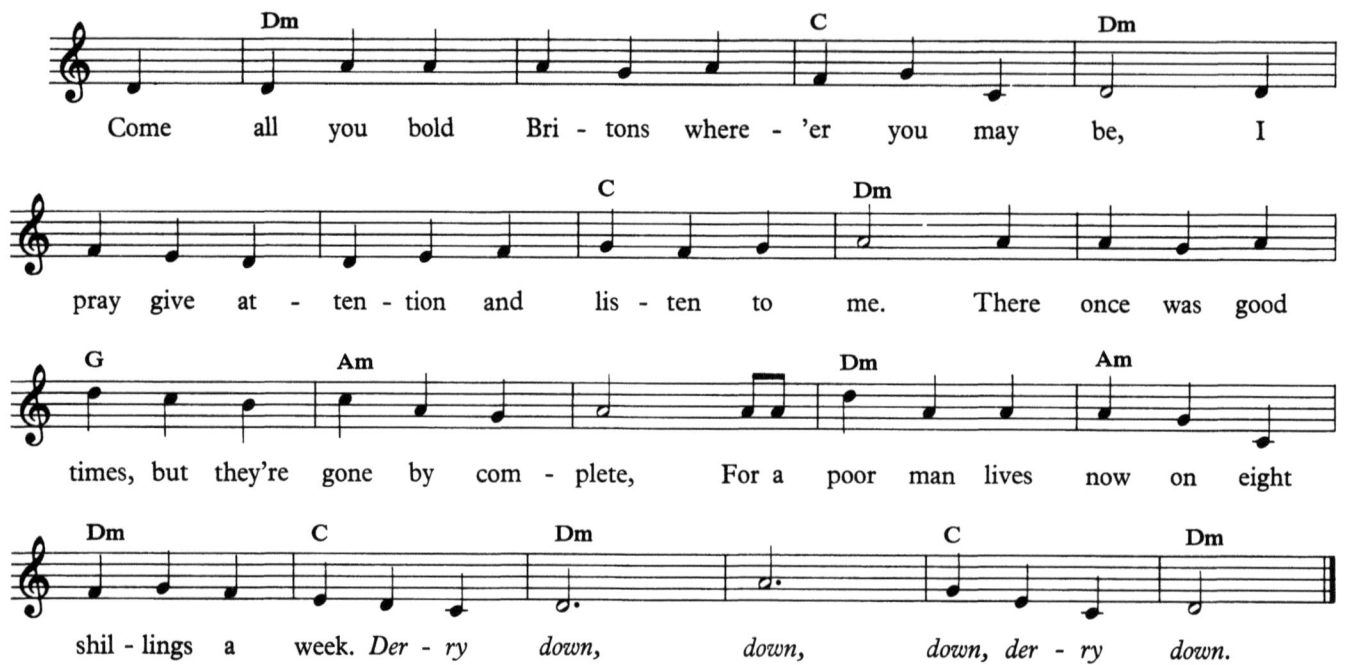

Come all you bold Britons where-'er you may be, I pray give attention and listen to me. There once was good times, but they're gone by complete, For a poor man lives now on eight shillings a week. Derry down, down, down, derry down.

2 Such times in old England there never was seen,
   As the present ones now, but much better have been.
   A poor man's condemned and considered a thief,
   And compelled to work hard on eight shillings a week.

3 Our venerable fathers remember the year,
   When a man earned three shillings a day and his beer.
   He then could live well, keep his family neat,
   But now he must work for eight shillings a week.

4 The Nobs of Old England, of shameful renown,
   Are striving to crush a poor man to the ground.
   They'll beat down their wages and starve them complete,
   And make them work hard for eight shillings a week.

5 A poor man to labour, believe me it's so,
   To maintain his family is willing to go
   Either hedging or ditching, to plough or to reap,
   But how does he live on eight shillings a week.

6 In the reign of old George, as you all understand,
   Then there was contentment throughout the whole land.
   Each poor man could live and get plenty to eat,
   But now he must pine on eight shillings a week.

7 So now to conclude and finish my song,
   May the times be much better before very long;
   May every labourer be able to keep
   His children and wife on twelve shillings a week.

Another account

In 1852, my first year out in service, I went as a carter's lad to Mr Pearce, Grove Farm, Peopleton. I was hired for the year and was paid thirty shillings. In the winter I had to be up to help the master chaff-cutting at 4 a.m., and often I was on shoe and knife and fork cleaning until 10 p.m. After that I went on to another farm called Ham Dean, for nine months at 2½d per day; then I was hired the next year [1854] for fifty shillings. My wages kept rising slowly after that until 1861. Then I married, and followed the occupation of a shepherd, and during a period of two years I received eight shillings per week of 'seven days'. Of course I had breakfast allowed me on Sundays mornings; and a cottage, 'Hovel', rent free, and two quarts of beer daily. Harvest wages were fifty shillings for the month, and dinner each day, and one got home at night with about enough time to prepare food and start off again for the next day's work. Between 1861 and 1872 my wages rose to eleven shillings a week, and then I was obliged, by the Education Act, to send seven of my nine children to school. I believe that it was in 1865 or 1866 that we paid 9d for the 4lb loaf. I do not think there are many people who would like to go back to the 'good old days' after all, although I am always thankful that it is not hard work that kills one. (Jesse Shervington, Iron Cross, Worcestershire, speaking in 1908, *Evesham NQ* II, pp. 221–2.)

Agricultural wages varied a good deal. In 1824, for example, they ranged from 4s 6d to 9s a week in the south and were higher in the north, the average being 9s 4d a week. Thomas Smart, in the same year, described his standard of life to a Parliamentary Committee:

He had had thirteen children, seven of whom were living, and the only parish relief he had ever had was for the burial of his children. By good luck and hard work, he had always enjoyed steady employment. In 1812, just before the depression, he had earned 12s a week: now it was 8s. At harvest he made an extra 40s, and three of his children earned between them 6s a week. He lived almost entirely on bread and cheese, had often touched no meat for a month, got now and then a little bacon and sometimes a halfpennyworth of milk, but the farmers did not like selling it. He had no pig, but did have a garden where he grew potatoes. House rent and fuel cost £5 a year, shoes 15s for himself and £1 for the family. (*Plenty and want*, p. 35.)

In the 1840s, according to Charles Robinson of Sussex, 'the usual wage for field work was 9s a week, and a half-gallon loaf of bread cost 1s 2d' (p.40). Robert Crick's family budget in 1843, with five people earning, was: Crick (aged 42), 9s a week; his wife (40), 9d; boy (12), 2s; boy (11), 1s; boy (8), 1s; two other children (6 and 4), not earning, total income 13s 9d a week; expenditure: bread 9s, potatoes 1s, rent 1s 2d, tea 2d, sugar 3½d, soap 3d, blue ½d, thread, etc. 2d, candles 3d, salt ½d, coal and wood 9d, butter 4½d, cheese 3d, total 13s 9d a week (p.45).

In the 1870s, wages had not always reached the 12s a week which the song (*Present times*) looked forward to. It was sung in the 1830s and 40s: between the Reform Bill and the Chartist agitations, as one critic puts it; and he adds that it reflects the views of the Tolpuddle martyrs, whose attempt to organise themselves and their fellows in a union branch led to their prosecution, conviction and transportation – and to national fame. When Joseph Arch set about organising his union in 1872, he remembered the men of Tolpuddle: 'Then I thought of what I was risking. I remembered the Labourers' Union in Dorsetshire, started in the thirties – what had become of that? Poor Hammett had had to pay a heavy price for standing up with his fellow labourers against the oppressors. He and five others had been tried in 1834, and sentenced to seven years' transportation. The plain truth of it was that, for daring to be Unionists they had been sent to the hulks in Australia'.

In March 1875, James Hammett was presented with a silver watch and an illuminated address, on behalf of the National Union of Agricultural Labourers.

Further reading
John Burnett, *Plenty and want*.
Cole & Postgate, *The common people*.
Joyce Marlow, *The Tolpuddle martyrs*, Deutsch 1971.

7
'It was 1835'

It was 1835, the winter of the Repeal of the Corn Laws.* I was about nine years old. I well remember eating barley bread, and seeing the tears in my poor mother's eyes as she cut slices off a loaf; for even barley loaves were all too scarce. About the time of the Repeal things had got so bad that they could hardly be worse. The food we could get was of very poor quality, and there was far too little of it. Meat was rarely, if ever, to be seen on the labourer's table; the price was too high for his pocket. In many a household even a morsel of bacon was considered a luxury. Flour was so dear that the cottage loaf was mostly of barley. Tea ran to six and seven shillings a pound, sugar would be eightpence a pound, and the price of other provisions was in

a man is bound to be a fast runner, agile and quickwitted. A man was often driven to poach, then, if he wanted to live. The plain truth is, we labourers do not believe hares and rabbits belong to any individual, not any more than thrushes and blackbirds do.

I have always been one for keeping the laws of the land and upholding them as far as possible; but how can I blame these men because they would not sit still, and let the life be starved out of them and theirs? They would not; so they risked their liberty, the next dearest thing they had – though it was a poor enough liberty at the best – in their endeavours to obtain food. The horrors of those times are clearly and vividly before my mind's eye even now. It is as if they had been burned and branded into me. I cannot forget them.

proportion. If fresh meat is still [1898] scarcer than it should be in the labourer's cottage today, he can at any rate get good wheaten bread and plenty of potatoes; but in the twenties and thirties he had neither wheaten bread nor a plentiful supply of potatoes to fall back on. They could not grow potatoes; they had no allotments then, they had no hope of them, and the bulk of labourers had no gardens.

As they were unable to procure fresh meat honestly, they stole that as well. Poaching became so prevalent that it is hardly an exaggeration to say that every other man you met was a poacher. It is my deliberate opinion that these men were to some extent justified in their actions; they had by hook or by crook to obtain food somewhere, in order to enable their wives and their children to live at all, to keep the breath in their bodies.

When I was a lad, there used to be a gang of poachers in our village; they went out at night as regularly in the seasons as others went to their day's work and their harvesting. There were, I believe, four or five, or maybe more, of them. One or two are still alive and following constant work; the others are old, or dead.

Poaching means very quick work, and, to succeed at it,

* If Arch really means 1835 – and if he were nine he could be speaking of no other year – he cannot mean the repeal of the Corn Laws, which took place in 1846. He probably means an agitation in favour of repeal. The farmers organised a petition in favour of the retention of the Corn Laws and Arch tells us that his father refused to sign, for which he was victimised by being kept out of work for eighteen weeks. The Corn Laws, first enacted in 1815, were designed to keep up the price of corn.

Song 11 *Van Dieman's Land*

Come all you gallant poachers, that ramble void of care,
That walk out on a moonlight night with your dog and gun and snare.
The hare and lofty pheasants you have at your command,
No thinking of your last career upon Van Dieman's Land.

2 Poor Tom Brown from Nottingham, Jack Williams and poor Joe,
We are three daring poachers, the country does well know.
At night we were trepanned by the keepers hid in sand,
Who for fourteen years transported us unto Van Dieman's Land.

3 The first day that we landed upon that fatal shore,
The planters they came round us, full twenty score or more.
They ranked us up like horses and sold us out of hand,
They yoked us unto ploughs, my boys, to plough Van Dieman's Land.

4 Our cottages that we live in are built of clod and clay,
And rotten straw for bedding, and we dare not say nay.
Our cots are fenced with fire, we slumber when we can,
To drive away wolves and tigers upon Van Dieman's Land.

5 It's often when in slumber I have a pleasant dream,
With my sweet girl a-sitting down beside a purling stream.
Through England I've been roaming with her at command,
Now I waken broken-hearted upon Van Dieman's Land.

6 God bless our wives and families, likewise the happy shore,
That isle of great contentment which we shall see no more.
As for our wretched females, see them we seldom can,
There's twenty to one woman upon Van Dieman's Land.

7 There was a girl from Birmingham, Susan Summers was her name,
For fourteen years transported, we all know well the same.
Our planter bought her freedom and married her out of hand,
She gave to us good usage upon Van Dieman's Land.

8 So all you gallant poachers, give ear unto my song,
It is a bit of good advice, although it is not long.
Throw by your dogs and snare, for to you I speak right plain,
Oh, if you knew our hardships, you'd never poach again.

Song 12 *The sheepstealer*

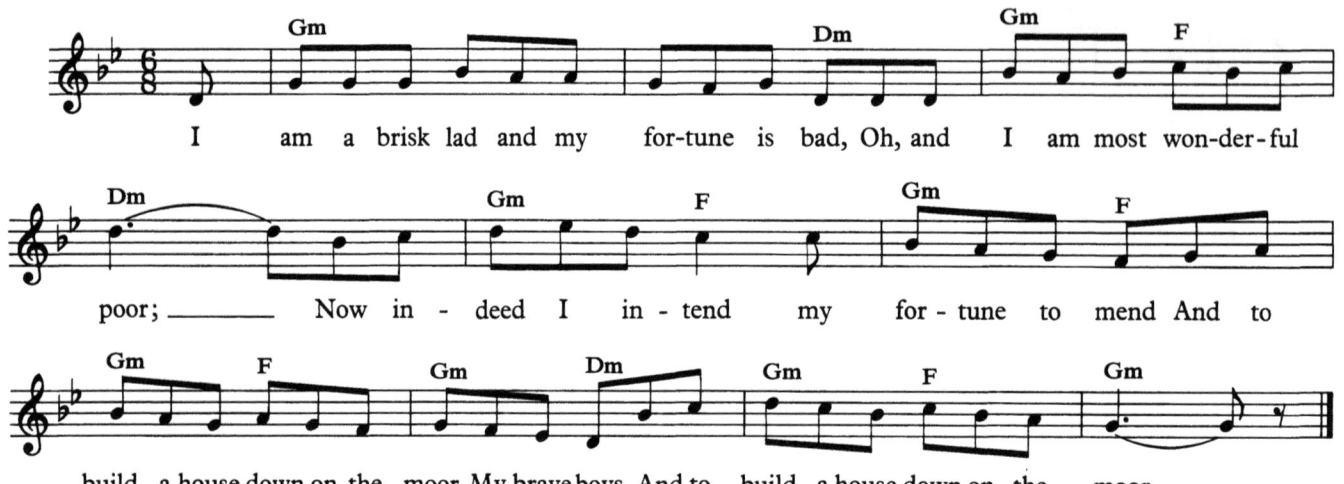

I am a brisk lad and my fortune is bad, Oh, and I am most wonderful poor; Now indeed I intend my fortune to mend And to build a house down on the moor, My brave boys, And to build a house down on the moor.

2 In my meadow I'll keep fat oxen and sheep
And a neat little nag on the downs;
In the middle of the night when the moon do shine bright,
There's a number of work to be done.

3 I'll ride all around in another man's ground
And I'll take a fat sheep for my own;
Oh, I'll end of his life by the aid of my knife
And then I will carry him home.

4 My children shall pull the skin from the ewe
And I'll be in a place where there's none;
When the constable do come, I'll stand with my gun
And swear all I have is my own.

Songs about poaching were extremely common, because poaching itself was so widespread. There is evidence of this in innumerable newspaper accounts of trials and frequent laws directed against poaching.

During the reign of George III (1760–1820), 32 new Game Laws were passed. The Act of 1800, for example, punished a first offender with hard labour, and a second (termed an 'incorrigible rogue') with whipping and two years' imprisonment or forced service in the army or navy. If an incorrigible rogue escaped from prison he was liable for transportation for seven years. This applied even to unarmed men, but was amended the following year to apply only to those who were armed. Such legislation was bitterly resented. The *Observer* newspaper published a letter sent anonymously to magistrates in 1816:

TAKE NOTICE: We have lately heard that there is an Act passed, that whatever poacher is caught destroying the game is to be transported for seven years. This is English liberty! Now do we swear to each other that the first of our company that this law is inflicted on, that there shall not be one gentleman's seat in our county escape the rage of fire (20 October).

The poaching bands continued to operate, certain of them being formed by ex-servicemen, after 1815, who used their military knowledge to perfect their campaigns. In companies of eighteen or twenty, they would confront the keepers in battle array.

Because of juries' reluctance to convict when they knew that a sentence of transportation was automatic, the law was changed in 1828. The penalties for poaching became three months' imprisonment for a first offence, six for a second, and transportation for a third. But if three or more men, one of whom carried a gun or bludgeon, were found in a wood, all were liable to be transported for fourteen years ('We are three daring poachers . . . for fourteen years transported').

Between 1827 and 1830, one in seven of all criminal convictions in this country was under the Game Laws. Cobbett remarked in 1826 that there were more persons imprisoned in England for offences against the Game Laws than in France, with more than twice the population, for all sorts of offences put together. At Winchester Lent Assizes in 1821, out of sixteen prisoners condemned to death, the only ones whose sentence was not commuted

Spring gun with brass cover, c. 1800. Spring guns were used against poachers in the early nineteenth century until they were made illegal in 1827

were two poachers. Mr Justice Burrough commented that 'It became necessary, in these two cases, that the extreme sentence of the law should be inflicted, to deter others, as resistance to gamekeepers has now arrived at an alarming height, and many lives have been lost'.

Of ninety-six prisoners for trial at Bedford in 1829, eighteen were poachers, including two brothers who had been unemployed. One, aged 22 and single, had been allowed 6d a day relief. The other, aged 28, married, with a pregnant wife and two children, had been allowed 7s a week. Both were hanged.

'Seven penn'orth' was slang for seven years transportation, so frequent had the punishment become. Newspaper accounts, like these, taken almost at random from *Berrow's Worcester Journal* were commonplace:

Issue for 6 March 1828

Thomas Bellamy, aged 31, and William Price, aged 36, charged with entering Hazle Wood, in the parish of Hadsor, the property of J. H. Galton, Esq., about midnight, on the 30th January, armed for the purpose of killing game. The prisoners belonged to a gang of five poachers, who violently assaulted Thoas. Shingles, Mr G.'s gamekeeper, and two assistants – seven years transportation.

31 April 1828

Removal of Convicts. Yesterday, the following convicts were removed from Worcester County Gaol; to Sheerness, to be transported for life: James Redding, for a robbery at Croome; Peter Dew, for a robbery at Leigh; Samuel Turnpenny and George Matty, for a robbery at Powick; James Roberts, for a highway robbery at Bewdley; Albert Whitehouse, for horse-stealing at Stanton Lacy; Joseph Checketts and Thomas Rook, for a robbery at Yardley; for fourteen years transportation: George Pope, for sheep-stealing at Kidderminster. To Woolwich, for seven years' transportation: John Hawkins and Thomas Jones, for poaching at Aldminster; Thomas Bellamy and William Price, for poaching at Hadsor; John Hall, for a burglary at South Littleton; and Joseph Moore, for a robbery at Stourbridge.

28 August 1828

Henry Munn, Francis Oseman, Maria Darke and Elizabeth Nutt were committed to hard labour at the tread mill, the first named for two months, the latter three for three months, as rogues and vagabonds. They were taken into custody on a charge of robbery, but the prosecutor did not appear.

9 April 1829

Warwick Assizes commenced on Monday, there were upwards of 200 prisoners for trial; six were charged with wilful murder; twelve with poaching and shooting with intent to kill: and thirty others with offences against the Game Laws.

23 April 1829

At the Warwick Assizes, judgement of death was recorded

against 66 prisoners, 28 of whom were poachers, found guilty of shooting at the gamekeepers of the Earl of Denbigh and D. S. Dugdale, Esq., M.P. At these Assizes there were 91 prisoners under 21 years of age.

Fierce passions were aroused in the struggle between poachers and authority. Man traps and spring guns were used against poachers. A shepherd in Warwickshire was skinned alive for having informed against poachers. Transportation to Van Dieman's Land went on until 1853 and to Botany Bay until 1857 but its terrible memory was present in the popular imagination for generations afterwards. G. E. Evans speaks of an out-of-the-way heath being called Van Dieman's Land and many outlying parts of parishes in Cambridgeshire and Suffolk being known as Botany Bay.

Poaching still went on, of course (and still does) and Joseph Arch was much concerned with the new Game Laws (see p. 45). G. E. Evans writes of poaching in the early years of this century:

The procedure does not vary greatly from county to county. A moonlit night was chosen and the poacher went with his gun to a remote part of an estate as unobtrusively as he could. From a previous expedition or a reconnoitre he had a rough idea where the birds roosted; but he approached the trees cautiously, looking round for any manholes that had been dug underneath the roost to trap nightwalkers like himself. When he was under the tree he fired his gun into the midst of the roosting birds, grabbing as many as he could as they dropped. He then ran from the spot as hard as he could go. (*Ask the fellows*, p. 183.)

Pheasants and hares were not the only animals taken. Sheep-stealing was also practised, but this was straight theft, rather than poaching, and punished even more severely:

It was not strange that sheep-stealing was one of the commonest offences against the law at that time [1830s], in spite of the dreadful penalty. Hunger made the people reckless. My old friend Joan, and other old persons, have said to me that it appeared in those days that the men were strangely indifferent and did not seem to care whether they were hanged or not. It is true they did not hang very many of them – the judge, as a rule, after putting on his black cap and ordering them to the gallows, would send in a recommendation to mercy for most of them; but the mercy of that time was like that of the wicked, exceedingly cruel. Instead of swinging, it was transportation for life, or for fourteen, and, at the very least, seven years . . . And some were hanged; my friend Joan named some people she knows in the neighbourhood who are the grandchildren of a young man with a wife and family of small children who was hanged at Salisbury. She had a vivid recollection of this case because it had seemed so hard, the man having been maddened by want when he took a sheep; also because when he was hanged his poor young wife travelled to the place of slaughter to beg for his body, and had it brought home and buried decently in the village churchyard. (*A shepherd's life*, p. 148.)

Further reading

Hammonds, *The village labourer*.
Cobbett, *Rural rides*.
Evans, *Ask the fellows*.
R. E. Moreau, *The departed village*, Oxford University Press, London 1968.
E. W. Bovill, *English country life, 1780–1830*, 1962.
E. W. Bovill, *The England of Nimrod and Surtees, 1815–1854*, 1959.
L. R. Haggard (ed.), *I walked by night*, Collins, 1935; reprinted Boydell Press, Ipswich, 1974.

8

'I stayed on in the old home'

I stayed on in the old home for a while [after the death of his mother, in 1842] and took care of my father, but I was more than ever bent on improving my condition and earning a better wage. A man from another part of the kingdom introduced a new style of hedge-cutting into our county. I very soon found out that he could make a tidy bit of money by it, so I set to work at once and learned how to do it.

Then hedge-cutting matches were 'hedging matches' they called them. The first time I competed I gained a prize; the second time I again won a prize; and the third time I carried off the first prize. Then a championship match was arranged, all the head prizemen for miles around being asked to compete. I entered the lists and won the first prize of two pounds, a medal, and the proud title of 'Champion Hedgecutter of England'.

Soon after this 'glorious victory', I went into different English counties, and also into Wales, hedge-cutting. I got good jobs and very good money, and was in great request. Not only was I a master of this branch of my craft, with men working under me, but, as I had taken to mowing when sixteen years of age, I had now become a master hand at that also, and had almost invariably a gang of from twenty to twenty-five men under me in the field. I made some very good mowing contracts with large graziers; they would give me six and seven shillings an acre. The farmers were not so liberal by half, as they seldom paid more than three shillings an acre.

It was in the early forties when I made my way back like a homing pigeon to the old Arch roof-tree. I was now a stalwart young man, nearing the end of my teens, a true chip off the old block. I had been journeying to and fro on the face of a fine broad bit of English earth, seeking what wages I could earn, what work I could get, and what facts I could devour. At the same time I was taking in a supply of facts which could not be digested – tough facts about the land and the labourer that accumulated and lay within my mind, heavy as a lump of lead, and hard as a stone.

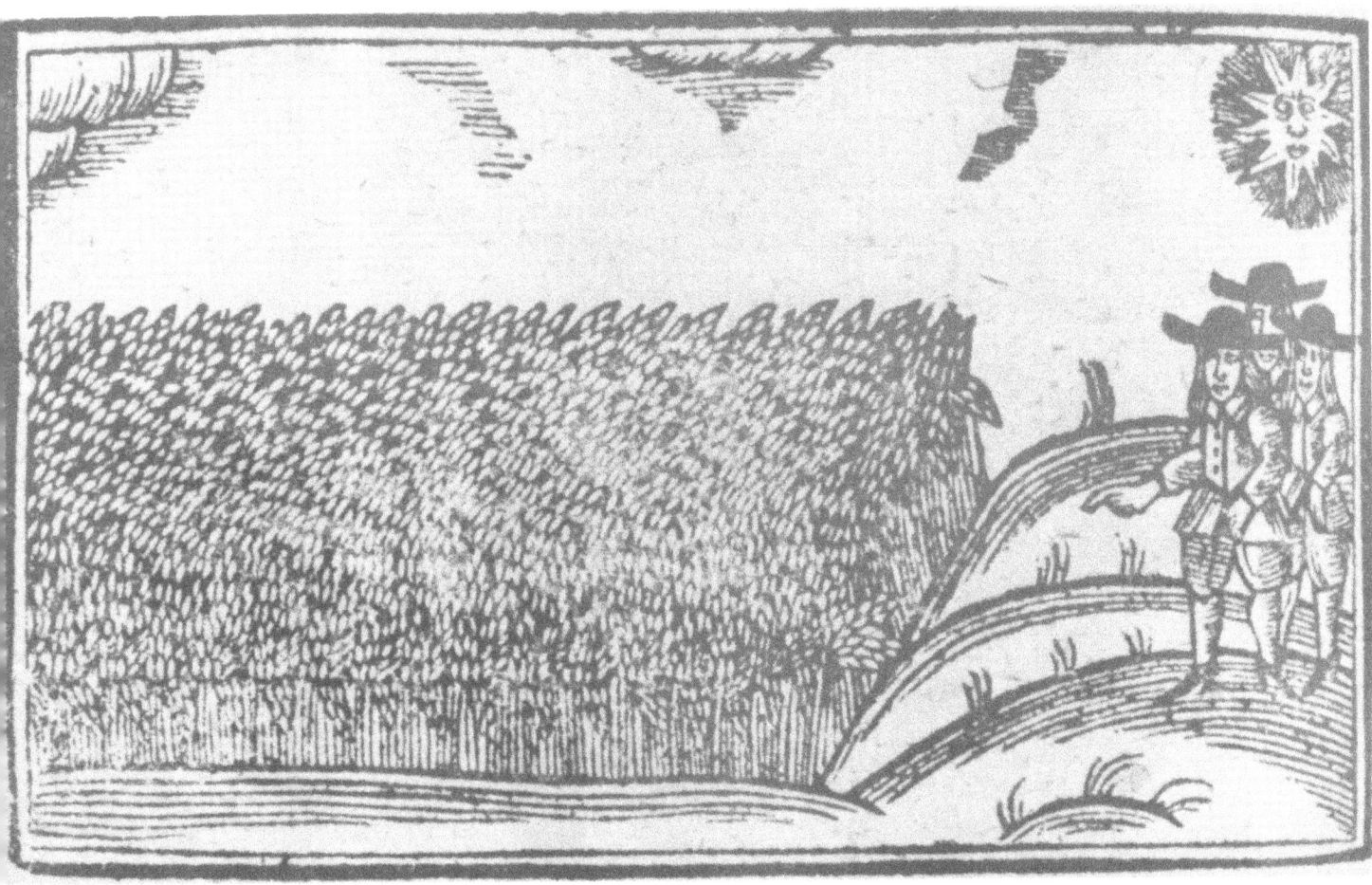

Song 13 *The rigs of the times*

2. Now the next is a baker, I must bring him in,
   He charge fourpence a loaf, he think it no sin;
   When he do bring it in, it's not bigger'n your fist,
   And the top of the loaf is popped up in the dish.

3. Now no wonder that butter be a shilling a pound –
   See the new farmers' daughters as they ride up and down –
   If you ask them the reason, they'll say, bonny lad,
   There's a French war† and our cows has no grass.

4. Oh, the next is a publican, I must bring him in,
   He charge fourpence a quart, he think it no sin;
   When he do bring it in, the measure is short:
   The top of the pot is popped up with the froth.

5. Now the very best plan that I can find
   Is to pop them all up in a high gale of wind;
   And when they get up the cloud it will bust
   And the biggest old rascal come tumbling down first.

* Stilyards (steelyards): primitive weighing machine.
† French war: the Napoleonic wars.

Song 14 *Poor shepherds*

2 Now the fields they are let out and the ditches tossed about,
And it's all for the sake of more gold.
With the posts and the rails we'll make them rakes and pails,
It will break the heart of every man.
And a-milking we must go, or follow the plough-tail.
To reap and plough and sow, aye, and to harrow we must go.

3 Now a poor man's pay is but eighteen pence a day;
You have need to double the price.
And what is that, d'ye think, to find them bread and drink,
Six children, the man and his wife?
Whilst the rich do play their cards, aye, the poor will all be starved,
To live on bread and water, don't you think it very hard?

* Boggins: hands; labourers.

A shepherd of 1836

During the mid-1840s, Arch saw 'smouldering discontent' among the labourers and looked forward to 'the day of wrath to come'. By his skill and enterprise he had managed to better his own condition, but this was the decade called the hungry 'forties, and the 'fifties were little better.

George Edwards, another farm labourer who became an M.P., was born in Norfolk in 1850:

At this time my father's wage had been reduced to 7s per week. The family was in abject poverty. When lying in bed with the infant [that is, George Edwards himself] the mother's only food was onion gruel. As a result of the bad food or, properly speaking, the want of food, she was only able to feed the child at her breast for one week. After the first week he had to be fed on bread soaked in very poor skimmed milk.

At the time of my birth my father was again a bullock feeder, working seven days a week, leaving home in the morning before it was light, and not returning in the evening until it was dark. He never saw his children at this time, except for a little while on the Sunday, as they were always put to bed during the winter months before his return from work. The condition of the family grew worse, for, although the Corn Laws were repealed in 1846, the price of food did not decrease to any great extent, but wages did go down. Married men's wages were reduced from 9s to 8s per week.

When the great Crimean War broke out in 1854, food rose to famine prices. The price of bread went up to 1s per 4 lb loaf, sugar to 8d per lb, tea to 6d per oz, cheese rose from 7d per lb to 1s 6d per lb. The only article of food that did not rise to such a proportionately high figure was meat, but that was an article of food which rarely entered a poor man's home, except a little piece of pork occasionally, which would weigh about $1\frac{1}{2}$ lb, and this would have to last a family of nine for a week.

The only thing which did not rise to any great extent was wages. My father was taking 8s per week of seven days. I was then four years of age and the hardships of those days will never be erased from my memory. My father's wages were not sufficient to buy bread alone for the family by 4s per week. In order to save the family from starvation, my father, night by night, took a few turnips from his master's field. These were boiled by my mother for the children's supper. The bread we had to eat was meal bread of the coarsest kind, and of this we had not half enough. We children often used to ask this loving mother for another slice of bread, and she, with tears in her eyes, was compelled to say she had no more to give. (*From crow-scaring to Westminster.*)

Further reading

Hudson, *A shepherd's life*.
Evans, *Ask the fellows* (chapters on bread and beer).
George Edwards, *From crow-scaring to Westminster*, London, 1922, reprinted 1957.

9
'In 1847'

In 1847, when barely one-and-twenty years of age, I took unto myself a wife. We soon settled down comfortably in the cottage, where seven children were born to us, six of whom are still living.

By this time I had formed my political opinions. When I was only about eighteen years of age, I made up my mind to be a Liberal, and I have stuck to the party ever since. I expect the Tory barley bread I had to feed on got into my bones and made me a Liberal. It has had that contrary effect on more than one man I have come across.

The stage of my life on which I had now entered was a busy, a varied, and a trying one. I was determined that my children should be brought up decently; that they should have plenty of plain wholesome food; as good an education as I could get them and give them; and a fair start in life. So I set off on my travels. Hard work, good wages, rough quarters, strange companions, long journeys and long absences – such was the programme. When in Wales I would preach in chapels among the mountains, and more than once I have 'held forth' in my everyday clothes. Working, preaching, and reading whatever books or papers I could pick up, I would find my way home and settle down for a while to much the same kind of life in the village.

All this disputing and contending with the high and mighty ones helped to spread my name abroad, and there was not a parson or a squire in the countryside who loved the sound of it.

Song 15 *Prop of the land*

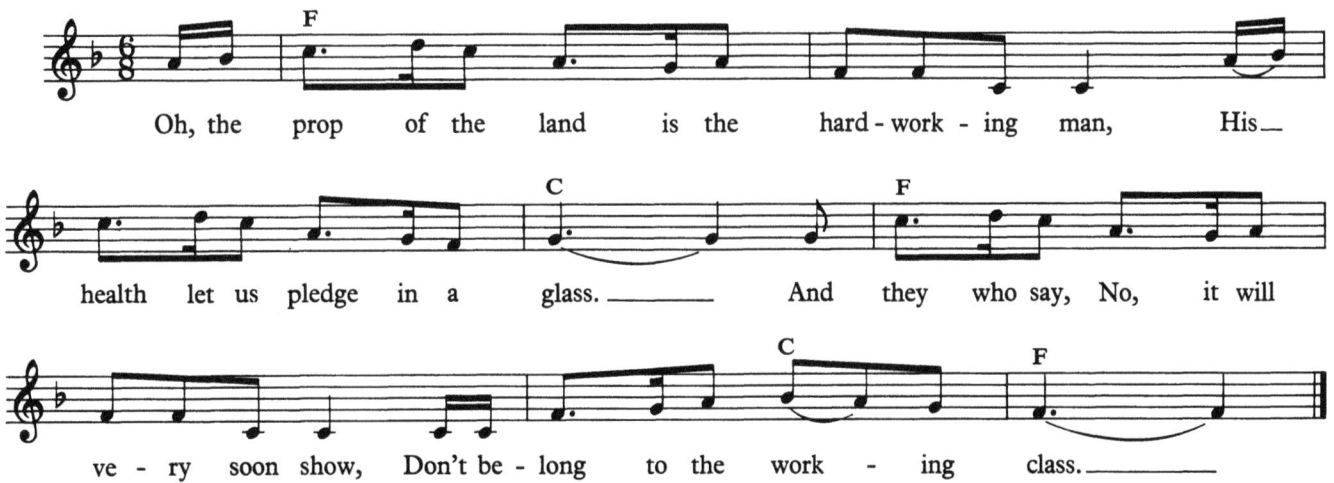

Oh, the prop of the land is the hard-working man, His health let us pledge in a glass. And they who say, No, it will very soon show, Don't belong to the working class.

2 Is it the rich man that supports the land?
He looks on while the poor man must work.
The poor man must toil with his hard brown hand
From daylight until dark.

3 Those rich grinding knives would have us poor slaves,
And take from the poor man what he earns.
You hear them boast how they rule the roast,*
And the poor man they treat like a worm.

4 Why should the rich man despise us, the poor,
When we toil for him hard, night and day?
The time it will come when the rich man will die,
And beside the poor man he must lay.

5 For death lays low both great and small,
And if life was a thing we could buy,
The rich man would give his thousands to live,
While the poor man he might die.

Repeat the first verse

* Rule the roast: be master (now usually 'rule the roost').

10

'By the end of the sixties'

By the end of the sixties and the beginning of the seventies, I had bettered my position as a labourer all round. I did not work then for farmers at ten shillings a week! I used to obtain large ploughing jobs at from two shillings to three-and-sixpence a day; but the farmers would cut me down to two shillings whenever they could. I also used to get work as a carpenter's labourer, then my skill at hurdle-making and gate-hanging would come in handy at odd times. Being a good all-round man I was never at a loss for a job.

But, if things were going well with me at the beginning of the seventies, they were going from bad to worse with the agricultural labourer generally. In our part of the country his poor little tide of prosperity was at its lowest ebb. Things were so bad with the men that they were beginning to grow desperate. The trodden worms, which had so long writhed under the iron heel of the oppressor, were turning at last. The smouldering fire of discontent was shooting out tongues of flame here and there. The men were murmuring and muttering the countryside round, but they wanted a voice; they spoke low among themselves, but they were afraid to speak out. They were sick of suffering but they had no physician. I took note of it all; I had been taking note of it for years; and I thought out the remedy, and that was *Combination*.

After the harvest of 1871 had been reaped, and the winter had set in, the sufferings of the men became cruel, and when the new year of 1872 opened there seemed to be only two doors left open for *them*: one was the big door of disgrace which led to a life of degradation in the poor-house; the other was the narrow door of death, which perchance would lead to a freer and happier life beyond the grave. When such a choice as this was all that was left for many an honest labouring man, who will dare to blame them because they refused to make it! Their poverty had fallen to starvation point, and was past all bearing. They began to raise their heads and look about them; and they saw that if they would keep life in their bodies, and rise out of their miserable state, they must set to and force open a door of escape for themselves. Oppression, and hunger, and misery, made them desperate, and desperation was the mother of the Union.

Song 16 *The fine old English labourer*

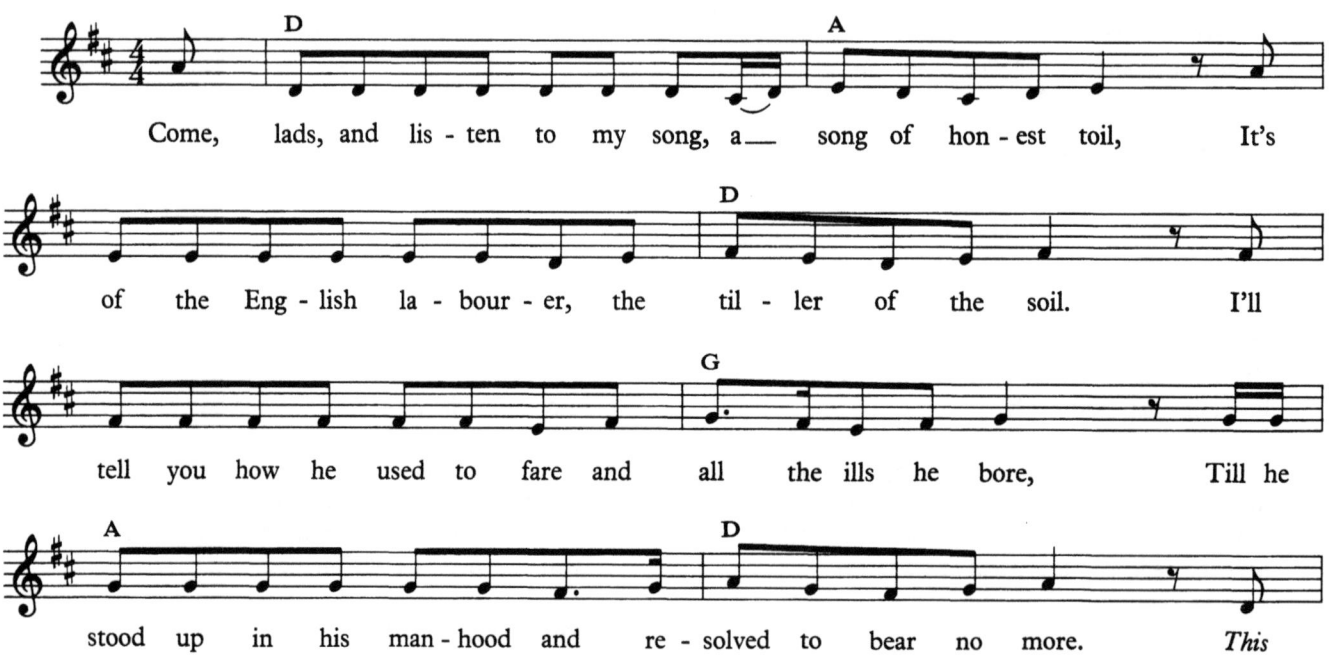

fine old English labourer, one of the present time.

2 He used to take whatever wage the farmer chose to pay,
   And work as hard as any horse for eighteenpence a day;
   Or if he grumbled at the nine and dared to ask for ten,
   The angry farmer cursed and swore and sacked him there and then.

3 He used to tramp off to his work while town folk were abed,
   With nothing in his belly but a slice or two of bread.
   He dined upon potatoes and he never dreamed of meat,
   Except a lump of bacon fat sometimes by way of treat.

4 He used to find it hard enough to give his children food,
   But sent them to the village school as often as he could.
   But though he knew that school was good, they must have bread and clothes,
   So he had to send them to the fields to scare away the crows.

5 He used to walk along the fields and see his landlord's game
   Devour his master's growing crops and think it was a shame,
   But if the keeper found on him a rabbit or a wire,
   He got it hot when brought before the parson and the squire.

6 But now he's wide awake enough and doing all he can
   At last, for honest labour's rights, he's fighting like a man.
   Since squires and landlords will not help, to help himself he'll try,
   And if he does not get fair wage, he'll know the reason why.

7 They used to treat him as they liked in the evil days of old,
   They thought there was no power on earth to beat the power of gold;
   They used to threaten what they'd do whenever work was slack,
   But now he laughs their threats to scorn with the Union at his back.

This song was well-known to Arch and he quoted it in full in his autobiography. It was written by Howard Evans, another union leader, and was often sung at meetings. Arch comments: 'If a squire or a parson or a farmer had passed by on the other side while we were singing this song or others like it, his ears would have told him that the English labourer was awake to his wrongs, and meant to have his rights at last. Yes, poor Hodge was sitting up and rubbing his eyes after his long sleep.'

It is a parody of a song well-known at the time, called *The fine old English gentleman*, and it gives a remarkably detailed and accurate picture of the lives of farm labourers, not only for 1882, but in some respects for much longer periods of the nineteenth century.

'He used to take whatever wage': Arch used almost the very words as late as 1882 of labourers in some parts of England ('they have been obliged to take whatever wage the farmer chose to pay'). 'Eighteenpence a day', or 9s a week, was the wage of many labourers; 'twelve shillings was the average (in 1872), and there were men getting nine and ten shillings; and some were earning on an average not more than eight', says Arch. 'A slice or two of bread': this is confirmed, not only by Arch's account but by others (see p. 42). 'To scare away the crows': Arch himself did this and it was the general practice to send children to work as early as possible in order to supplement the family income. G. E. Evans writes: 'The farmers wanted cheap labour and the parents wanted money; and these two facts conspired to keep many children out of school when they should have been at their desks. In fact many of them must have spent as much time working on the land as they did at school'. (*Ask the fellows*, p. 174.)

'He got it hot': although the Game Laws were no longer as savage as they had been earlier in the century (see pp. 34 ff), magistrates were still hard on poachers. Arch tells of a man 'who most brutally ill-treated his wife. The punishment he got was a fine of ten shillings and costs. In the very same place, and just a week after, a man was brought up for poaching, and he was fined one pound and costs'. The Poaching Prevention Act of 1862 empowered a constable to search any labourer on suspicion of poaching, and the power, according to Arch, in his evidence to the Parliamentary Select Committee on the Game Laws, in 1873, was frequently abused. 'They used to treat him as they liked': one aspect of life in which this applied – and still does, in some cases – was the tied cottage, from which the labourer might be 'kicked out bag and baggage, at a week's notice, if Dives so chose'.

The main feature of the song, however, is the new spirit of defiance which characterised the early days of the new labourers' union.

Further reading

Evans, *Ask the fellows*.

Mowers, 1802

11

'The day was 7th February, 1872'

The day was 7th February, 1872. It was a very wet morning, and I was busy at home on a carpentering job; I was making a box. My wife came in to me and said, 'Joe, here's three men come to see you. What for, I don't know'. But I knew fast enough. In walked the three. They said they had come to ask me to hold a meeting at Wellesbourne that evening. They wanted to get the men together and start a Union directly.

I remember that evening, as if it were but yesterday. When I set out I was dressed in a pair of cord trousers, and cord vest, and an old flannel jacket. As I tramped along the wet, muddy road to Wellesbourne my heart was stirred within me, and questions passed through my mind and troubled me. Was it a false start, a sort of hole-and-corner movement, which would come to nothing, and do more harm to the men than good? If a Union were fairly set afoot, would the farmers prove too strong for it?

When I reached Wellesbourne, lo, and behold, it was as lively as a swarm of bees in June. We settled that I should address the meeting under the old chestnut tree; and I expected to find some thirty or forty principal men there. What then was my surprise to see not a few tens but many hundreds of labourers assembled; there were nearly two thousand of them. The news that I was going to speak that night had been spread about; and so the men had come in from all the villages round within a radius of ten miles. Not a circular had been sent out nor a handbill printed, but from cottage to cottage, and from farm to farm, the word had been passed on; and here were the labourers gathered together in their hundreds. Wellesbourne village was there, every man in it; and they had come from Moreton and Locksley and Charlecote and Hampton Lucy, and from Barford, to hear what I had to say to them. By this time the night had fallen pitch dark; but the men had got bean poles and hung lanterns on them, and we could see well enough.

A meeting under the Wellesbourne Tree

I mounted an old pig-stool, and in the flickering light of the lanterns I saw the earnest up-turned faces of these poor brothers of mine – faces gaunt with hunger and pinched with want – all looking towards me and ready to listen to the words that should fall from my lips. These white slaves of England stood there with the darkness all about them, like the Children of Israel waiting for someone to lead them out of the land of Egypt.

We passed a resolution to form a Union then and there, and the names of the men could not be taken down fast enough; we enrolled between two and three hundred members that night.

Joseph Arch

Thomas Parker

Edwin Russell

William Lewis

Joseph Arch and some of his colleagues from the early days of the Union, 1872

Song 17 *My master and I*

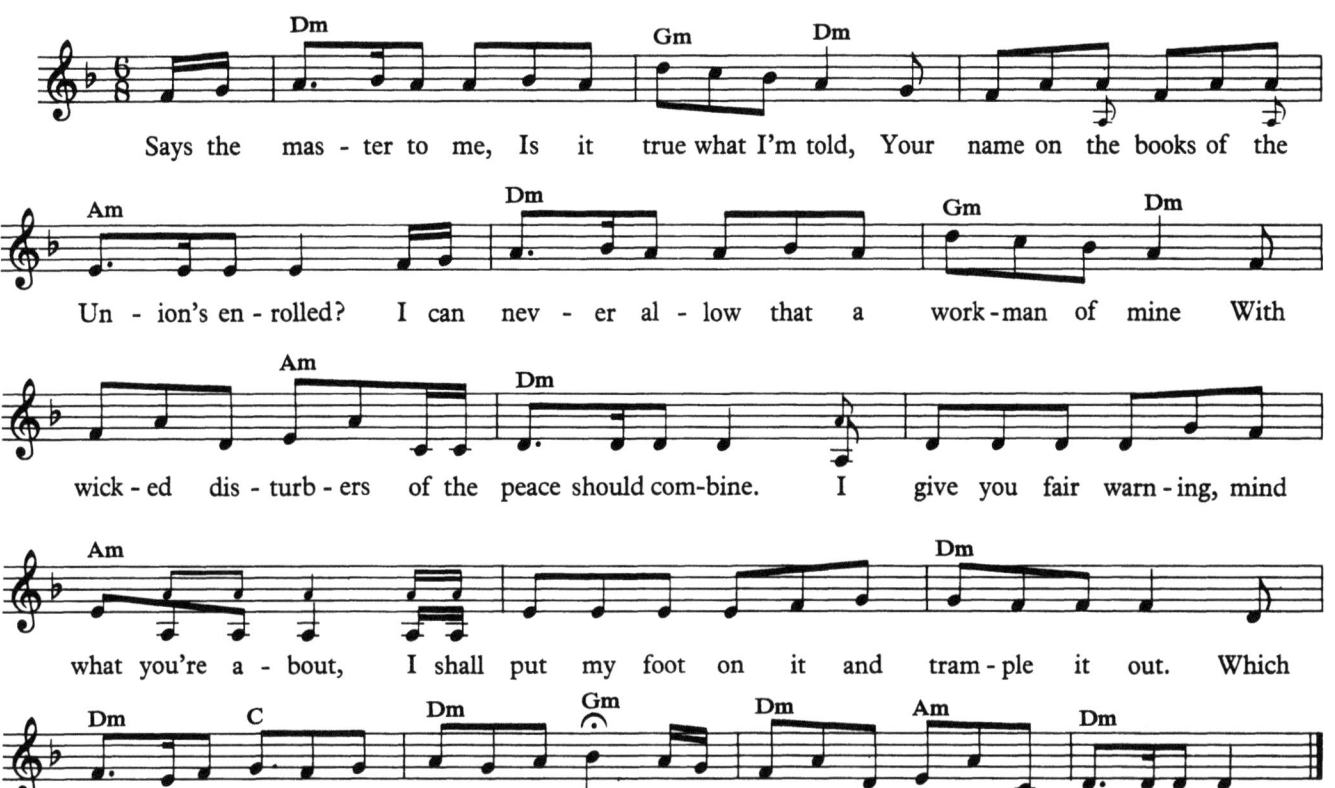

Says the master to me, Is it true what I'm told, Your name on the books of the Union's enrolled? I can never allow that a workman of mine With wicked disturbers of the peace should combine. I give you fair warning, mind what you're about, I shall put my foot on it and trample it out. Which side your bread's buttered, I'm sure you can see, So decide now, at once, for the Union or me.

2 Says I to my master, It's perfectly true
That I'm in the Union, and I'll stick to it, too.
And if between Union and you I must choose
I've plenty to win and I've little to lose.

3 For twenty years mostly, my bread has been dry,
So to butter it now I shall certainly try,
And though I respect you, remember I'm free
No master in England shall trample on me.

4 Says the master to me, Just a word or two more;
We never have quarrelled on matters before.
If you stick to the Union, 'ere long I'll be bound,
You'll come and ask me for more wages all round.

5 Now I can't afford more than two bob a day,
When I look at the rent and the taxes I pay,
And the crops are so injured by game as you see;
If it's hard for you, then it's hard for me.

6 Says I to the master, I do not see how
Any need has arisen for quarrelling now,
And though likely enough we shall ask for more wage,
I promise you we shan't get first in a rage.

7 Here comes Mr Taylor, so stout and so bold,
The head of the Labourers' Union, I'm told.
He's persuaded the men to stick up for their rights,
And they say he's been giving the farmers the gripes.

The news that a union was to be formed was like a declaration that a new era had dawned. Arch went round spreading the gospel to enthusiastic audiences. This is an account of a meeting in February 1872. A labourer is speaking.

Listen! He is seventy years of age. He has been a farm labourer sixty-three years, having begun when he was barely seven. He has preserved his character; he has worked hard except in times of sickness, he has kept off the parish; his master and the squire and the parson give him a good word. He has given sons and daughters to the state. Of the lads, the bones of one are whitening in India, where he fell; another sleeps with his comrades in the English cemetery at the Crimea; a third was lost at sea; one or two yet remain, and they are on the soil.

This man deserves well of his country; and the country recognises his deserts to the extent of paying him eleven shillings a week, stipulating that he shall work for this from dawn to dark. He knows that, for the last twenty years, taking one week with another, 'he ant earned so good as eleven shillin'! He is now old and very soon he will have to stand by. What awaits him then? 'A bit o' stone-breakin' on the roads, two shillin' a week from the parish, and a loaf or two'.

He reads in the papers as 'ow the country's growin' richer and richer' and thinks summut should be doin' for th' lab'rin' class. He has no hope for himself, but afore he dies he'd uncommon like to see the young uns doin' better nor he's done. He's heered o' the Wellesbourne men, and Muster Arch, and seein' as th' master and th' squoire canna greatly harm him, sin' he's nigh done, he's made bold to ax Muster Arch to come and tell em down here what they must do to get a trifle more wage and a bit better food; and Muster Arch, like a good un as he is, has come, and will speak to um himself!

Tremendous cheering, amid which Joseph Arch rises in the waggon and faces the crowd. These men before him, and all of their class, have any quantity of faith in him. They call him 'our man, our Joe, the labourers' hope, apostle, friend.' Look at him as he stands there eyeing the crowd, the light full upon his face. Brow broad and open; eyes frank and brave; chin square and firm; face browned with exposure and marked with small-pox, but thoroughly honest and manful; head round, very well set.

'I shall perhaps do right at the outset if I tell you I am a working man – one of yourselves. I am come here tonight to explain to you what is the great necessity of the day with regard to the working man. There is a great, deep necessity, which must soon be met. I know of efficient, able-bodied men who only get 10s a week. Lately I went to the house of an old experienced shepherd, whom I found with his wife in a hovel not fit to turn pigs in, and the poor old man, who works from five in the morning till seven or eight at night, only receives 5s a week and two loaves. Only yesterday, a waggoner told me he works from four in the morning till eight at night, except on Sundays, when he works from five till six. The man works one hundred hours in the seven days for 12s 6d, or 1½d an hour. I want to ask every sensible individual how it is possible for a man with four or five children to support them decently, respectably, and properly on 12s a week. The working man needs more money, and must have more. Let us claim our rights with English independence, honesty and manhood.' (Written by the Rev. F. S. Attenborough, a Congregational minister of Leamington; published in A. Clayden, *The revolt of the field*.)

In March a letter was sent to all the farmers in the district: Sir, We jointly and severally request your attention to the following requirements – namely 2s 8d per day for our labour; hours from six to five; and close at three on Saturday and 4d an hour overtime. Hoping you will give this your fair and honest consideration.

The farmers ignored the letter and there began several years of strikes and lockouts, which achieved a 55 per cent increase in the average of the labourers. The struggle was hard.

On the following Saturday [after the letter], when the men went for their money, they found the farmers obdurate – so they decided to come out on strike. Two hundred farm labourers struck work. Some farmers came to terms, but the majority of them refused to attempt a compromise and resorted to coercive measures, in some cases evicting the labourers and their families from their homes. So accustomed had the farmers grown to the shocking condition in which their men had always existed, that they never dreamt these same men would have strength enough to revolt.

When the men realised that the men were not to be broken, the landowners as well as the farmers began to victimise Union men. Notices were served on them to quit their cottages. In numerous instances labourers had the brutal choice put before them to give up the Union or quit their employment and be ejected from their cottages. Respectable, industrious men, who had dwelt in cottages for many years and paid their rents regularly, were turned out at a week's notice for refusing to leave their Union. (Josiah Sage, *Memoirs*.)

Further reading

Clayden, *Revolt of the field*, 1874.
Sage, *Memoirs*, 1951.
R. Groves, *Sharpen the sickle – the history of the farm workers' union*, Porcupine Press, London 1949.

12

'At one place, forty-five men gave in their names'

At one place forty-five men gave in their names, and a branch was formed in less than five minutes. The movement spread on and on, into no less than eight counties. The men of Oxfordshire, Herefordshire, Leicestershire, Somersetshire, Norfolk, Northampton, Essex and Worcestershire rose to their feet in their valleys of dry bones, and stood up for the Union. Then the whole country was aroused and ringing with the news. All the leading papers took note of this strange thing; they could no longer ignore the fact that a great moral and intellectual awakening was in progress among the down-trodden peasantry of England.

There was anger and amazement among the powers of the land – the lord, the squire, the farmer, and the parson – when they saw these serfs of the soil girding on their manhood, and heard them refuse to starve any longer on nine and ten shillings a week.

The movement was flowing over the country like a spring tide. The men of Denham in Buckinghamshire joined in hundreds. There was agitation in Norfolk, where the men struck for shorter hours; there was a lock-out at Long Sutton Marsh, and very soon the wages in the district advanced to two shillings and threepence and two shillings and sixpence a day. Men in Dorsetshire were striking; the labourers about Shaftesbury and Blandford came out asking for a rise to twelve shillings a week. The state of the labourer in that county was as bad as it very well could be.

The men of Gloucestershire and Worcestershire were moving and meeting. The wages there were from nine up to twelve shillings a week, and I dare say the average would be about ten shillings. Rents were high, from four to six pounds a year, and the accommodation was miserable. They worked very long hours all over this part. A man would start at five o'clock in the morning, and he did not leave off until dark; often he was at it till very late, and cases were frequent where men had a day's work that went nearly round the clock twice over.

At one meeting I asked the men who were not in debt to the shop-keeper to hold up their hands, and when I looked there was not one single hand held up.

Labourers' strike meeting in the 1870s

Song 18 *Come all you bold fellows that follow the plough*

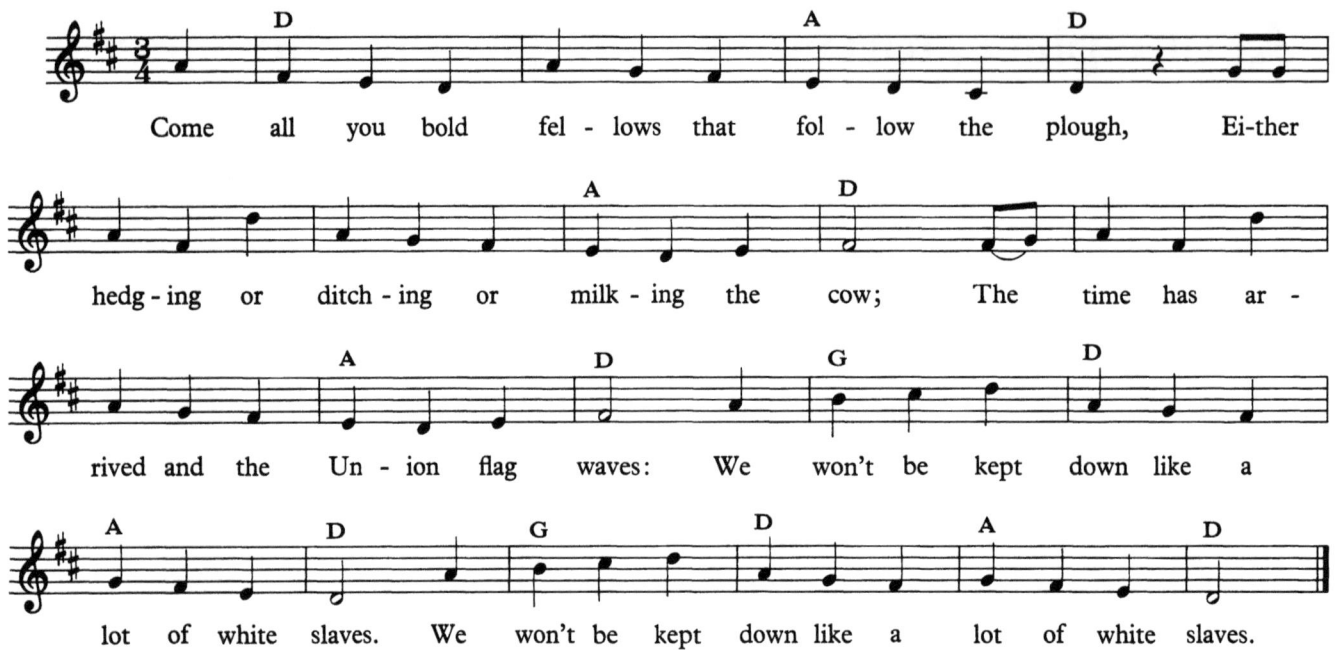

Come all you bold fellows that follow the plough,
Either hedging or ditching or milking the cow;
The time has arrived and the Union flag waves:
We won't be kept down like a lot of white slaves.
We won't be kept down like a lot of white slaves.

2 From Langport and Martock we'll meet at Stoke Cross,*
For the fat-bellied farmers we don't care a toss,
From Odcombe and Preston and Montacute too,
We'll come with flags flying and ribbons of blue.

3 You may now tell the farmers you'll be slaves no more;
The starvation wages you will not endure.
Though you worked night and day, you could not satisfy,
They treated you worse than a pig in a sty.

4 The farmers will very soon find I am sure
That a man is a man if he's ever so poor,
And no better man can in England be found
Than the hard-working man who is tilling the ground.

5 All England will learn of our doings today,
As in grand procession we all march away;
And the down-trodden labourers will cry as they march,
May God bless our hero, the brave Joseph Arch.

* The place names are in Somerset.

In March the Warwickshire Agricultural Labourers' Union was inaugurated and, in May, this, together with union branches from twenty-five other counties, became the National Agricultural Labourers' Union, with Joseph Arch as chairman. The secretary was Henry Taylor, a carpenter co-opted for his experience as a trade unionist (see the reference to him in the song on p. 49). In June the *Labourers' Chronicle* was launched, to give the movement a voice.

Arch stumped the country to gain support and the union had 100,000 members by the end of 1872. 50,000 were organised in rival unions. (There were 650,000 agricultural labourers.) He went to Tysoe, 13 miles from Wellesbourne, in July:

Arch was known to one or two Tysoe men. He was like themselves, only more powerful, a leader. He was a champion hedge-cutter, a travelling piece-worker, and a Methodist preacher. The labourers were uplifted because a few score of their own sort had shown themselves men and one was a prophet, but they expected the prophet's voice to be lost in the wilderness.

Josiah Smith opened the meeting. It was his own life he told of – a hungry childhood, no schooling, a crowded cottage. In thirty-five years' time will his sons have the same tale to tell? It looks as if they will. For the labourer things have stood still. What of other folk? Farmers' wheat prices have risen; the Marquis's [of Northampton] rents have trebled. Yes, trebled.

His audience knew and gave the answers (to his questions). Did y'ever hear of a little un dying o' wakeness? – Ah, that we did. An' what's t'other word for it? – Starvation. And did y'ever hear o' the red ribbon took from a little gal's hair, and her told to tell her mother not to dress her above her station? – What do they pay a lad of fifteen, fit t'eat an ovenful of bread as a lad is then? – Give him a man's work and half a man's starvation pay.

Then Arch rose. He had never suffered starvation! That was true. For him this was not a protest about his own conditions; he could earn his living anywhere in England. No, he spoke of the misery of his fellows, the unnecessary misery; the work-house future, the denial of manhood to labourers, the down-thrusting of their children. It was time the labourers stood firm for their rights.

Arch had no poetry, no rhetoric, but his voice was full and clear, reaching far beyond the limits of the crowd, thrown back now and then from the houses and even from the hills beyond in a fine echo.

(At this point, the Vicar, who was in the audience, called out, asking to be allowed to speak. There were some navvies present, who were working on the new railway line from Stratford to Fenny Compton Junction, and they made a move to duck the Vicar in the pond, but he was protected by the labourers and allowed to speak.)

The Vicar began. Arch and his like were stirring up mischief. Some of Josiah's facts he admitted (the stranger's speech he would ignore). He himself, some years back had paid eight shillings as a wage. (Shame! groans the audience. It didn't pay the baker, called a shrill woman's voice.) But things had improved; wages had gone up by a shilling a week. The audience groaned again. I myself, he said, have obtained allotments for you. A voice went on with the Vicar's sentence: At two pounds an acre, and let them to you at four. (*Joseph Ashby*, pp. 57ff.)

Lock-outs, strikes and evictions continued, but the union's efforts in 1872 and 73 were successful. However, in 1874, farm prices began to fall and farmers made a big effort to smash the union. Despite help from trade unionists in cities like Birmingham and Manchester, the union was defeated and went into decline, which was accelerated by disunity and internecine struggles. There was something of a revival in 1890, but this was stopped by a deepening of the depression in 1891 and 1892. By 1896, agricultural trade unionism was dead. It was not resuscitated until 1906, when George Edwards became secretary of an East Anglian union which later developed into the present body, the National Union of Agricultural and Allied Workers. In launching the new union, Edwards wrote: 'The men have been disorganised for ten years, and in consequence their condition is no better than it was prior to 1872. But if such an effort [to form a union] is to be successful, one thing is essential. There must be no rival Unions. The many rival Unions that were raised in Arch's days were, I have no doubt, a great factor in its fall.'

Further reading

Edwards, *Crow-scaring to Westminster*.
Sage, *Memoirs*.
L. Birch, *The history of the T.U.C. 1868–1968*, published by the T.U.C., London 1968.
Groves, *Sharpen the sickle*.

13

'In my own county'

In my own county it was reported in the spring of 1879 that there were over a hundred farms to let, amounting to a twelfth part of the entire county. I could not help feeling that this agricultural depression was a natural judgement on the farmers for their treatment of the labourers. They had, in their criminal folly, recklessly cast from them the best men – and a good farm-hand is a very good thing. This is what Thorold Rogers said at a meeting we held at Oxford in 1878: 'Let me say a word or two about the functions of a first-class farm-hand, and I am quite certain that there are many in this room who will agree with me. Suppose I ask a man whether he thinks it is an easy thing to drive a straight furrow over a ten-acre field, and to carry his furrow from one end of the field to the other, and from this side to that without any "wobbling" in his work. What would he say? Why it is as hard work as painting pictures. Let me ask you about shearing a sheep. It is a much easier task to clip a boy's head at a barber's shop than to shear a sheep, and nothing is more artistic than a clean, well-sheared sheep. Then how about rick-building. You may depend on it that it is, on the whole, harder to build a rick well than a house well.

'I have spoken about three high arts possessed by a good farm-hand. Now, how about making a ditch and a hedge! This is no easy matter; and it requires a considerable amount of skill to be able to make a line straight across a fifty-acre field, and to do it to the particular point, having laid the drain-pipes in such a way as not to allow a break in the outfall of water.'

Song 19 *The painful plough*

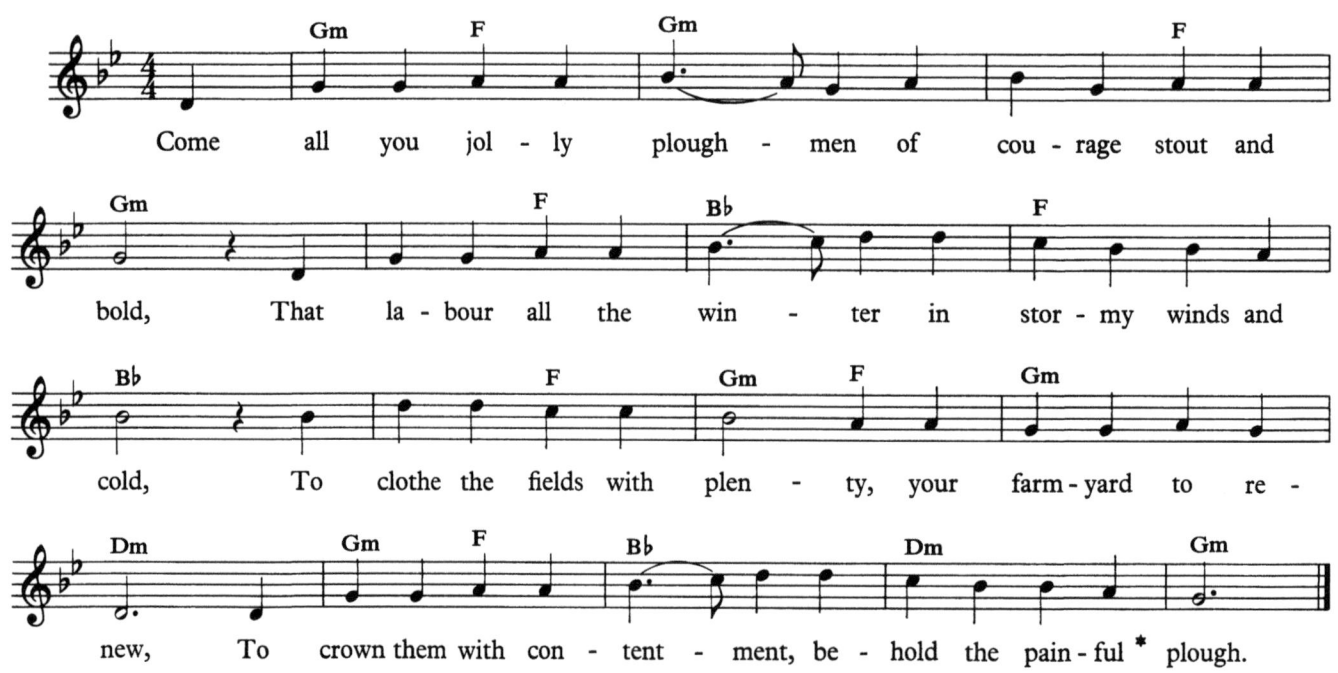

2   For Adam was a ploughman when ploughing first begun,
     The next that did succeed him was Cain the eldest son;
     Some of the generation the calling now pursue,
     That bread may not be wanting remains the painful plough.

* Painful: laborious.

3 Now Samson was the strongest man, and Solomon was wise,
   Alexander for to conquer was all his daily prize,
   King David he was valiant, and many thousands slew,
   Yet none of these brave heroes could live without the plough.

4 Behold the wealthy merchant that trades in foreign seas,
   And brings forth gold and treasure for those that live at ease,
   With finest silks and spices, and fruits and dainties too,
   They are brought from the Indies by virtue of the plough.

5 For they must have bread, biscuit, rice pudding, flour and peas,
   To feed the jolly sailors as they sail o'er the seas,
   Yet ev'ry man that brings them here will own to what is true –
   He cannot sail the ocean without the painful plough.

'Ye gen'rous Britons. Venerate the Plough.' An engraving of *1801*

Song 20 *The sheep shearing*

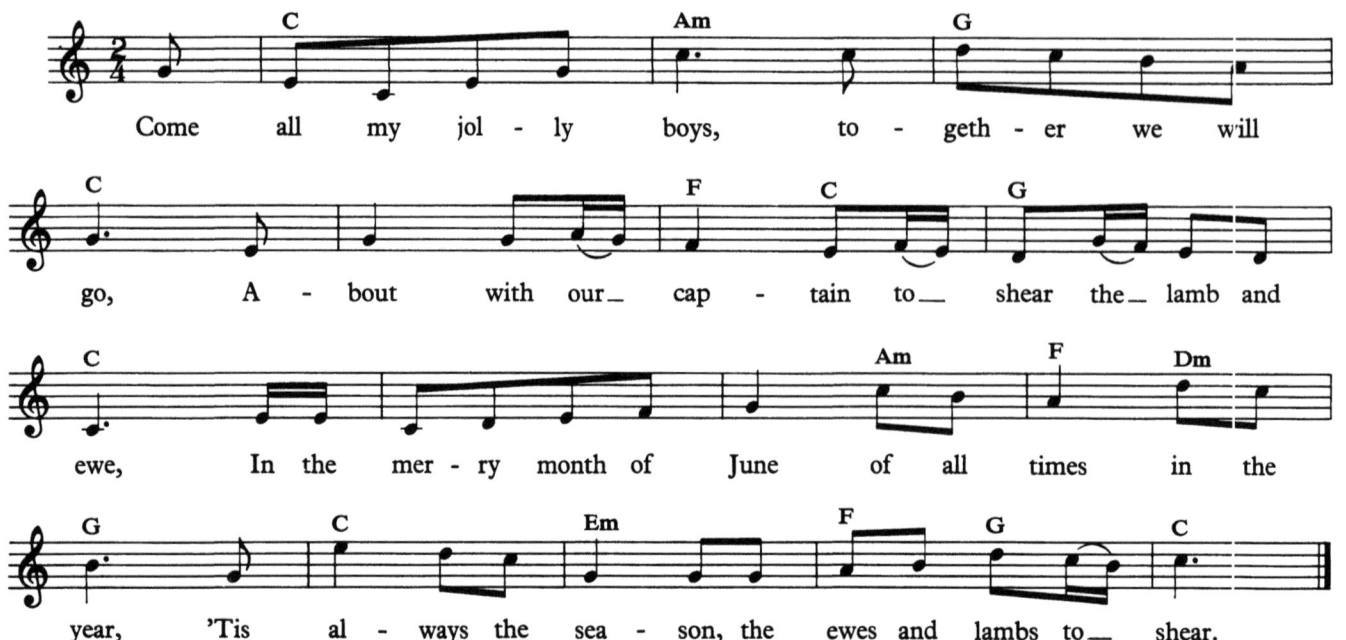

Come all my jolly boys, together we will go, About with our captain to shear the lamb and ewe, In the merry month of June of all times in the year, 'Tis always the season, the ewes and lambs to shear.

2 And then we must work hard, until our backs do ache;
   Our master he do bring us beer whenever we do lack;
   Our master he comes round to see our work is doing well:
   He cries, Shear them close, men, there is but little wool.

3 And then our noble captain doth to our master say,
   Come, let us have one bucket of your good ale, I pray.
   He turns unto our captain and makes him this reply:
   You shall have the best of beer, I promise, presently.

4 And when 'tis night and we have done our master is more free,
   And stores us well with good strong beer and pipes and tobaccee;
   So we do sit and drink, we smoke and sing and roar,
   Till we become more merry, far, than e'er we were before.

5 When all our work is done and all our sheep are shorn,
   Then home to our captain to drink the ale that's strong;
   'Tis a barrel then of wine cup we call the *Black Ram*,
   And we do sit and swagger and swear that we are men.

6 But yet before 'tis night, I'll stand you half a crown
   That if you have a special care the *Ram* will knock you down.
   What comes from butt will go to butt, so all you have a care:
   Don't lose your head, nor lose your wool, when you the sheep do shear.

Shearing time

According to certain historians, agriculture went through a period of great prosperity during the period from 1850 to 1874. This may have been true for the squires and farmers, but, to judge from their songs, it was not true for the labourers on whom the entire edifice rested.

The prosperity of the 'Golden Age' came to a sudden end in 1874 when, for the first time, Free Trade exposed English agriculture to the world's grain and meat producers, and from this time until 1896 there followed a period of almost uninterrupted depression, deepened at times by domestic catastrophes such as bad harvests and cattle plagues. With great stretches of land going out of cultivation and much more under-cultivated, the immediate effect of the agricultural crisis on the worker was to reduce the demand for labour and to lower wages, sometimes by 1s, occasionally by 2s, a week; not surprisingly, the rural exodus continued at an increased momentum, and farmers complained that with the departure of their best labourers they now had to pay more to get the same quantity of work done. A witness before the Royal Commission on Agricultural Depression of 1882 summed up the effects accurately when he said, 'I should say that the landlord suffers least . . . that the farmer suffers most, but that he feels his suffering less than the labourer. To the labourer it is a question really of less food, to the farmer it is not absolutely a question of bread, it is comforts or no comforts.' (*Plenty and want*, pp. 166–7.)

The tide in wages and conditions did not begin to turn again until the last years of the century and this was a time when many traditional songs like *The painful plough* were taken down from country singers. Most ploughing was still being done in 1900 by three-horse plough teams, with a boy walking beside the horses and a man at the plough-tail. In the course of ploughing an acre, which was considered to be one day's work, they walked eleven miles as they drove their nine-inch furrow. The ploughman and the shepherd were still the aristocrats of the labouring community and songs like this helped to uphold their dignity during the long years of depression.

Further reading

Evans, *Ask the fellows*.
G. E. Evans, *The horse in the furrow*, Faber, London 1967.
B. Kerr, *Bound to the soil, a social history of Dorset, 1750–1918*, John Baker, London 1968.
Burnett, *Plenty and want*.
J. Burnett, *A history of the cost of living*, Penguin Books, Harmondsworth 1969.
Moreau, *The departed village*.
Flora Thompson, *Lark rise to Candleford*, Oxford University Press, London 1965.
Copper, *A song for every season*.
F. E. Huggett, *A day in the life of a Victorian farm worker*, Allen and Unwin, 1972.
F. E. Huggett, *A short history of farming*, Macmillan, 1970.
J. Ray, *British agriculture*, Nelson, 1973.
R. Blythe, *Akenfield*, Penguin, 1972.

Shepherds, 1642

14

'The day I entered Parliament'

The day I entered Parliament as Joseph Arch, M.P. for North-West Norfolk, was a proud one. Joseph Chamberlain and Jesse Collings were my sponsors. I did not put on a black coat – I aped nobody – I wore my rough tweed jacket and billy-cock hat; the same I generally wore at my country meetings.

I rose to make my maiden speech on 26th January 1886. in which I opposed Mr Chaplin's Allotment Bill.

The fact was, I considered 'three acres and a cow' all moonshine. The Allotments Act was a miserable failure until the labourers got the vote, but since then thousands of acres have been put into their hands.

Labourer and milkmaid, 1802

The Reform Act of 1884 gave farm labourers the vote and Joseph Arch was elected to Parliament the following year, as a Liberal. There were a number of schemes afoot at the time to give land to the labourers, in the shape of smallholdings and allotments. The *Labourers' Chronicle*, for example, wanted the gradual expropriation of land held by charities and corporations, the confiscation of 10 per cent of every gift or legacy of land exceeding 100 acres, and the division of the resultant area into smallholdings. Henry Taylor went even further, and argued that 'the land of this country is held of the Queen for the good of the people, and if that trust is forfeited the land must revert to the people'.

It seems that the labourers, their union shattered and their hopes of immediate betterment defeated, took refuge in wild, utopian ideals – millenarianism. One such scheme was propounded by Jesse Collings, one of the Birmingham M.P.s, and his programme for smallholdings was briefly famous under the slogan of 'three acres and a cow'. Arch called it 'moonshine' when he wrote his autobiography, but at the time, he campaigned in favour:

He was speaking in a very large tent, crowded with people, at the time of Jesse Collings' 'three acres and a cow' agitation. Some man who had just got his head into the doorway thought he would floor Arch, and shouted at the top of his voice, 'Where are your three acres and the cow, guv'nor?' And in an instant came the retort from Arch, 'Oh, the cow will soon be here right enough, the calf is bellowing in at the doorway there'. (Sage, *Memoirs*, p. 49.)

Song 21 *Three acres and a cow*

2. There's a certain class in England that's holding fortune great,
   As give a man such a starving wage to work on their estate.
   The land's been stolen from the poor and those that have it now,
   They do not want to give a man three acres and a cow.

3. D'y' think they'd ever want to give three acres and a cow
   When they can get a man to take low wage to drive the plough?
   To live a man he has to work from daylight until dark
   So the lord can have both bulls and cows a-grazing in his park.

4. But now there is a pretty go in all the country through;
   The working men they want to know what the gov'ment it will do;
   And what we have been looking for, I wish they'd give us now:
   We're sure to live if they only give three acres and a cow.

5. If all the land in England was divided out quite fair,
   There would be work for every man to earn an honest share.
   Well some have thousand acre farms which they have got somehow,
   But I'll be satisfied to get three acres and a cow.

15

'As I sit here'

As I sit here in my little cottage at Barford [1898] and review the past, it seems at one minute a long look back; at another it seems but yesterday when my grandmother sat in the chair I am sitting in now – a chair which is over a hundred years old – and I stood by her, a little chap of six. And there is the old eight-day clock which my father bought in Leamington more than fifty years ago. He, I have heard him tell, carried home the case over his shoulder, and my mother trudged at his side with the works in her market basket. I can see my good mother cutting the barley bread for us, with tears in her eyes because there is so little of it for the children who are so hungry. I can see my father step in at the door, come home from his work for a bite and a sup of whatever is going. I can see myself tramping off in my little smock-frock, clapper in hand, to scare away the birds; then jumping the clods at sixpence a day; and so on, right away on to the great year of 1872 when I held that first meeting under the Wellesbourne chestnut-tree on the February evening which saw the birth of the Agricultural Labourers' Union.

Medieval wood-carving (misericord) in the church at Ripple, Worcestershire, showing sowing and harrowing

Song 22 *The jolly ploughboy*

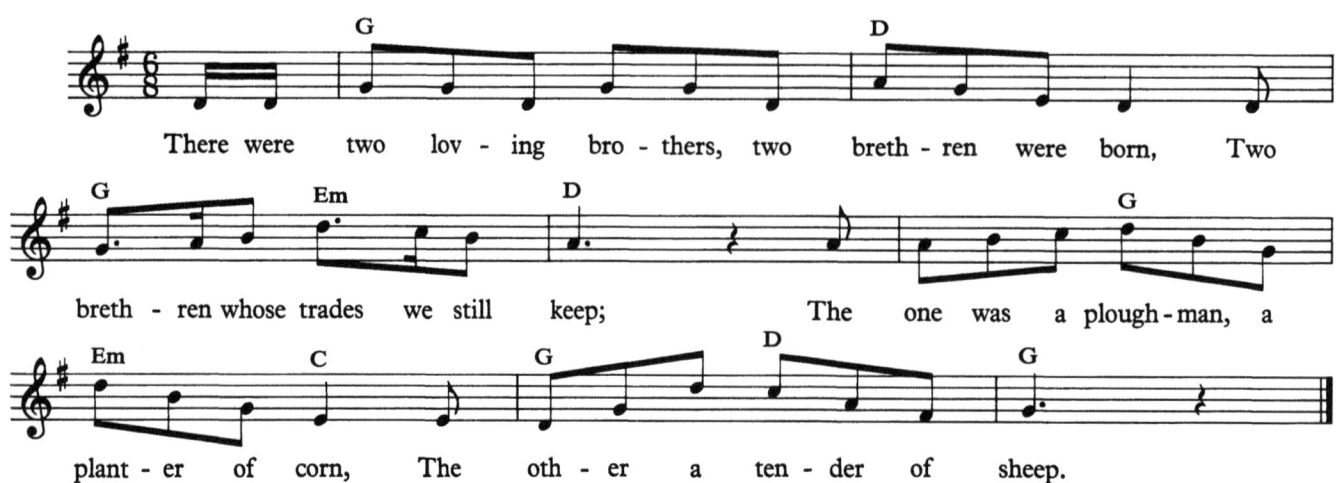

There were two loving brothers, two brethren were born,
Two brethren whose trades we still keep;
The one was a ploughman, a planter of corn,
The other a tender of sheep.

2 Here's April, here's May, here's June and July,
'Tis a pleasure to see the corn grow;
In August we moil it, shear low and reap high
And bind up our scythes for to mow.

3 So now we have gatherèd up every sheaf
And scrapèd up every ear;
We'll make no more to-do but to plough and to sow
And provide for the very next year.

4 Come all jolly ploughboys, come help me for to sing:
I'll sing in the praise of the plough,
For though we must labour from summer to spring,
We all will be merry boys now.

5 We've hirèd, we've mirèd through mire and through clay,
No pleasure at all could we find;
Now we'll laugh, dance and sing, and drive care away,
No more in this world to repine.

Joseph Arch retired in 1900 and died in 1919 at the age of 92. After the break-up of the union he had formed, he was not a popular figure with the labourers whom he had led, and 'at one time he was walking the streets of London, an M.P., with scarcely a penny in his pocket' (Sage). Yet, as he looked back on his career, the highest point was not his election to Parliament but the day in 1872 when he 'stood up in his manhood and resolved to bear no more' (in the words of the song) and set out like a new Moses to lead the labourers out of Egypt.

Josiah Sage, who was born in 1870 and helped to re-form the union in 1906, knew Arch and profoundly respected him: 'Never before the days of Arch, nor yet since, have the ranks of the agricultural labourers produced such a man. He stood head and shoulders above his fellows.'

Sources of the Songs

1 **Bird scarers' cries**
   I: text: *Evesham Notes and Queries;* tune: F. Kidson, *Seventy-five British nursery rhymes,* n.d., p. 14.
   II: sung by Mr Greengrass, Aldington, Kent (*Journal of the English Folk Dance and Song Society,* 1944, p. 189).
   III: sung by Mr John Durbin, East Harptree, Somerset; collected by Cecil Sharp, April 1904 (*Journal of the Folk Song Society (JFS)*, II, p. 48); adapted.
   IV: sung by Mr John Rogers of Beaminster, Dorset (M. R. Dacombe, *Dorset up along and down along,* Dorchester, n.d. (1935), p. 40).

2 **The farmers done over**
   Text: broadside printed by Walker of Norwich (Bolingbroke Collection, Norwich Public Library); adapted. Tune (not indicated): *A-nutting we will go* (from the singing of Roy Palmer).

3 **Country hirings**
   Text: broadside printed by Harkness of Preston (Madden Collection, Cambridge University Library); abridged and adapted. Tune (not indicated): *The painful plough* (S. Baring-Gould, *Songs of the West,* 1895).

4 **The new-fashioned farmer**
   Text: broadside printed by Harkness of Preston (Madden Collection, Cambridge University Library); abridged and adapted. Tune, first four lines and chorus: sung by Mr John Denny (65), of Nevinton, Essex; collected by Ralph Vaughan Williams, under the title of *The old-fashioned farmer,* 25 April 1904 (BM Add. MSS 54187, II, bk IV 124).

5 **The sucking pig**
   Text: broadside printed by Wright of Birmingham (Broadsides in folder marked 'religious' in map cabinet drawer 50, Birmingham Reference Library); abridged. Tune, under the title of *The tythe pig,* sung by R. Hard, South Brent, Devon; collected by S. Baring-Gould (*Songs of the West,* no. 29).

6 **The labouring man**
   G. Hill, *Wiltshire folk songs and carols,* Bournemouth, 1904, no. 3, 'from Durrington, near Stonehenge'; slightly adapted.

7 **Pity poor labourers**
   Text: broadside printed by Hanson of Northampton (Madden Collection); adapted. Tune (not indicated): by John Swift, based on *The ploughman,* sung by Henry Burstow, Horsham, Sussex; collected by Ralph Vaughan Williams, 1904 (*JFS* II, p. 190).

8 **The Owslebury lads**
   Sung by Mr James Stagg, Winchester, Hampshire; collected by G. B. Gardiner, 1906 (MS. H 204, Cecil Sharp House); slightly adapted.

9 **The honest ploughman**
   W. A. Barrett, *English Folk-Songs,* n.d. (1891), p. 32.

10 **Present times, or Eight shillings a week**
   Text: J. Ashton, *Modern street ballads,* 1888, p. 192. Tune (not indicated): *Come all you young sailors,* sung by Mr Donger, King's Lynn, Norfolk; collected by Ralph Vaughan Williams, 13 January 1905 (*JFS* II, p. 171). The refrain has been added with the melody.

11 **Van Dieman's Land**
   Text: broadside published by Catnach of London (Broadsides in folder marked 'miscellaneous' in map cabinet drawer 50, Birmingham Reference Library). Tune: sung by Mr Anderson, King's Lynn, Norfolk; collected under the title of *Young Henry the poacher* by Ralph Vaughan Williams, 9 January 1905 (*JFS* II, p. 166).

12 **The sheepstealer**
   Collected in Dorset by H. E. D. Hammond (*JFS* VII, pp. 87–8).

13 **The rigs of the times**
   Sung by John ('Charger') Salmond at *The Windmill,* Sutton, Norfolk; collected by E. J. Moeran, 1947 (BBC Recorded Programme Library). A simplified version of the tune has been given. One line of the text has been collated with a broadside of the same title (Ballad Collection BR F 04 BA 1, p. 196, Manchester Reference Library).

14 **Poor shepherds**
   Sung by Mr Matthew Hunt, Sherborne, Dorset; collected by H. E. D. Hammond, July 1906 (*JFS* VII, p. 85); adapted.

15 **Prop of the land**
   Sung by Robert Goodwin, Southrop; collected (text only) by Alfred Williams, about 1914 (*Folk songs of the Upper Thames,* 1923, p. 105; reprinted by S. R. Publishers, 1971). Collated with broadside, *Here's a health to the hard-working man,* printed by Such of London (Bolingbroke Collection). Tune (not indicated): a version of *Little Sir Hugh* (source not traced).

16 **The fine old English labourer**
   Written by Howard Evans, to the tune of *The fine old English gentleman.* The text was published in Evans' *Songs for singing at agricultural labourers' meetings* (Leamington, n.d.) and became very popular at union meetings. The tune which stems from a seventeenth-, century original, was widely used for political songs. Our version is from E. Duncan, *The minstrelsy of England,* n.d. (1905), vol. II, p. 207.

17 **My master and I**
   Written by Howard Evans, to the tune of *Bonnie Dundee.* Text published in Evans, op.cit.; final verse added from broadside, published by Such of London (Kidson Coll., Mitchell Library, Glasgow).

18 **Come all you bold fellows that follow the plough**
   Written by a Mr Reader; communicated by Mr D. Price, Head of History, Stanchester County Secondary School, Stoke-sub-Hamdon, Somerset. Tune (not indicated): *The carter's song,* sung by Mr Grantham (73), Anstie, Holmwood, Surrey; collected by L. E. Broadwood, February 1892 (*JFS* V, p. 271).

19 **The painful plough**
   Barrett, op.cit., no. 3, 'a North Country song'; abridged.

20 **The sheep shearing**
   Barrett, op.cit., no. 14. 'This is a Sussex sheep-shearing song, still sung at Shoreham at the proper season'; abridged.

21 **Three acres and a cow**
   Text: broadside printed by Brooks of Bristol (Broadsides in folder marked 'political' in map cabinet drawer 50, Birmingham Reference Library); adapted. Tune: *I wish they'd do it now.*

22 **The jolly ploughboy**
   H. Sumner, *The besom makers,* 1888, p. 23.

Sources of Illustrations

Page 10 British Museum, Roxburghe Ballads, I, 155; **p. 11** misericord, Ripple church, Worcester, by permission of the Vicar; **p. 16** BM, Roxburghe Ballads, I, 121; **p. 17** William Hone's *Everyday book*, photograph Cambridge University Library; **p. 18** haymaking, BM, Roxburghe Ballads, II, 80; **p. 19** Staffordshire porcelain, County Museum, Truro, Cornwall; **p. 21** broadside ballad, Birmingham Reference Library; **p. 23** cartoon, 1831, photograph Mansell Collection; **p. 27** cartoons of the Labourers' Revolt of 1830–1, Mansell; **p. 29 and cover** from G. Mitchell, *The Skeleton at the plough*, 1874, photo BM; **p. 30** broadside ballad, Kidson Collection, Mitchell Library, Glasgow; **p. 31** cartoon from *Punch*, 1843, photo Mansell, **p. 33** BM, Bagford Ballads, II, 155; **p. 34** woodcuts from broadside ballads, Madden Collection, Cambridge University Library; **p. 37** Museum of Science and Industry, Birmingham; **p. 38** broadside, London University Library; **p. 39** BM, Roxburghe Ballads, II, 80; **p. 42** from A. Gossett, *Shepherds of Britain*, 1911, photo Cambridge University Library; **p. 46** mowers 1802 from W. H. Pyne, *Microcosm*, 1803, photo Cambridge University Library; **pp. 47, 48, 51** Mansell Collection; **p. 55** from Cunnington & Lucas, *Occupational Costume in England*, photo Cambridge University Library; **p. 57** from A. Gossett, *Shepherds of Britain*, 1911, photo Cambridge University Library, **p. 58** BM, Tract 188, Thomason Collection, II, photo Cambridge University Library; **p. 59** from W. H. Pyne, *Microcosm*, 1803–7, photo Cambridge University Library; **p. 61** misericord, Ripple church, Worcestershire, reproduced by permission of the Vicar.

List of records

The painful plough, Topic Impact IMP-A-103 (produced by Roy Palmer; includes the following songs from this book: nos. 2, 3, 5, 7, 8, 9, 10, 13, 14, 15, 17, 19, 20).
Waterloo-Peterloo, Argo DA 86, nos. 6 and 11. No. 11 occurs on at least three other records: *Fair game and foul*, Topic 12T195, *You rambling boys of pleasure*, Topic 12T269, and *A proper sort*, Leader LED2063.
The sweet primroses, Topic 12T170, no. 13.
The Manchester Angel, Topic 12T147, nos. 12 and 22.
A song for every season, Leader LED2067, no. 20.

Drama

R. Leach, *The Wellesbourne Tree*, Blackie, Glasgow, 1975, is a musical documentary play on the life of Joseph Arch and the foundation of the National Agricultural Labourers' Union. Songs from this book are among those included.

Index of Songs

(*first lines are shown in italics*)

All you that love a bit of fun 20
Away, you black devils, away 9
Bird scarers' cries 9
Come all my jolly boys 56
Come all you bold Britons 32
Come all you bold fellows that follow the plough 52
Come all you bold young country lads 15
Come all you gallant poachers 35
Come all you jolly husbandmen 28
Come all you jolly ploughmen 54
Come all you swaggering farmers 12
Come, lads, and listen to my song 44
Country hirings 15
The farmers done over 12
The fine old English labourer
Gee, hallo, hallo, blackie cap 10
Good people, all draw near 41
Good people all, I pray attend 14
Hey, shoo all the birds 10
The honest ploughman 28
I am a brisk lad 36
The jolly ploughboy 62
The labouring man 22
My master and I 49
The new-fashioned farmer 14
O, you nasty black-a-tops 9
Oh, the prop of the land is the hard-working man 43
Oh, 'tis of an old butcher 40
The Owslebury lads 25
The painful plough 54
Pity poor labourers 24
Poor shepherds 41
Present times, or Eight shillings a week 32
Prop of the land 43
The rigs of the times 40
Says the master to me 49
The sheep shearing 56
The sheepstealer 36
The sucking pig 20
There were two loving brothers 62
The thirtieth of November 25
Three acres and a cow 60
Van Dieman's Land 35
You Englishmen of each degree 22
You sons of old England 24
You've heard a deal of talk 60

For EU product safety concerns, contact us at Calle de José Abascal, 56–1°,
28003 Madrid, Spain or eugpsr@cambridge.org.

www.ingramcontent.com/pod-product-compliance
Ingram Content Group UK Ltd.
Pitfield, Milton Keynes, MK11 3LW, UK
UKHW051916230326
469290UK00012B/205